MARRAKESH by DESIGN

Decorating with All the Colors, Patterns, and Magic of Morocco

Maryam Montague

ARTISAN

NEW YORK

Published by Artisan
A division of Workman Publishing Company, Inc.
225 Varick Street
New York, NY 10014-4381
www.artisanbooks.com

Published simultaneously in Canada by Thomas Allen & Son, Limited

>>

Library of Congress Cataloging-in-Publication Data
Montague, Maryam.
  Marrakesh by design : decorating with all the colors, patterns, and magic of Morocco / Maryam Montague.
      p. cm.
  Includes index.
  ISBN 978-1-57965-401-6
1. Architecture, Domestic—Morocco. 2. Interior decoration—Morocco. 3. House furnishings—Morocco. I. Title.
  NK2087.75.A1M66 2012
  747.0964—dc23   2011035591

>>

Pattern illustrations by Melanie Royals, Royal Design Studio
Design by Susan E. Baldaserini

Printed in China
First printing, May 2012

10 9 8 7 6 5 4 3 2 1

For my parents,
who gave me the world,
and for my husband,
who came with me to explore it.

Contents

Preface   6

An Introduction: Morocco and Moroccan Style   12

PART I   **DISCOVERING MOROCCAN STYLE**

Chapter 1   Exploring Architecture   20

Chapter 2   Understanding Features and Finishes   42

Chapter 3   Charting Color   66

Chapter 4   Uncovering Pattern   90

PART II   **LIVING MOROCCAN STYLE**

Chapter 5   Living and Dining Areas   114

Chapter 6   Bedrooms   138

Chapter 7   Kitchens, Baths, and Transitional Spaces   158

Chapter 8   Outdoor Living Spaces and Gardens   184

PART III   **SOURCING MOROCCAN STYLE**

Chapter 9   Shopping for Chic   214

Chapter 10   Finding Decor and Expertise   234

Acknowledgments   250

Index   253

Preface

I fell in love with Moroccan design ten years ago, and I have never looked back. In a world filled with beige interiors, Morocco seems the perfect antidote: a refuge for addicts of saturated color, a haven for devotees of intricate pattern, a destination for admirers of striking architecture. I thought I had stumbled upon Morocco accidentally, but perhaps the universe conspired to bring me there. Possibly North African style is part of my genetic makeup, as (by happenstance) I was born in Cairo to an American father and an Iranian mother. I am not sure of the exact reason, but I do know that my cravings for Morocco's spicy design mix were hard to resist. So I didn't: When a job opportunity arose, my husband (an American architect), my small son, and I moved to Morocco sight unseen.

Morocco is unlike any country I have ever known. We first lived in the capital city of Rabat, a leafy haven populated by diplomats and development workers. The weather is temperate and fine all year round. We immediately took to our life in Morocco; in fact, we liked it a lot. It starts with the people. Moroccans are kind and generous, apt to be interested in and helpful to foreigners who come their way. Although private and traditional by nature, Moroccans are quick to extend invitations for home-cooked meals or excursions into the souks. We spent our first weeknights with our new-found Moroccan friends, and our weekends taking road trips in our Land Cruiser. We passed memorable days in the imperial city of Fez, a short three-hour drive from Rabat. We roamed through the old city's narrow alleys and admired the famed blue-and-white pottery. We headed north into the Rif Mountains via curlicue passes that went up and up and up until we reached Chefchaouen, a large town entirely washed in blue lavender. We drank mint tea on the square and bought old Berber doors that we loaded on top of our car. We drove many hours south toward the Sahara and visited the cities of Ouarzazate, Zagora, and Merzouga. We photographed the casbah architecture in these places, with its mysterious tattoolike symbols carved into the walls, and we camped in the desert in handwoven Berber tents with proper beds set up inside.

After all our exploring of Morocco, it was Marrakesh that captured our attention the most.

We found ourselves making the four-hour journey over and over again to this city, which appears to spring like a mirage from a sea of palm trees. Marrakesh is populated with a large number of artists, designers, writers, photographers, and filmmakers. The old city, or medina, is extensive and bursting with beautiful things to look at, touch, and buy. There are pretty places to stay and chic restaurants to eat in. It has its own international airport with flights buzzing into and out of Europe. And so one fine day, we packed our bags and moved to Marrakesh. I started a blog, *My Marrakesh* (www.mymarrakesh.com), to chronicle our adventures.

It was not long before we fell under Marrakesh's spell and decided that our stay should not be temporary, but permanent. Perhaps it's the arches that cascade one after another or the mosaic tile that seems to stretch as far as the eye can see. I am not sure what it was that cast the spell, but suddenly our days were filled with real estate agents. A few short months after our search began, we signed the papers to purchase an olive grove in a little village outside of Marrakesh. My husband got to work designing three pavilions in a modern Moroccan architectural style, with domes, a spiral staircase, and a small casbahlike tower. We named our place Peacock Pavilions after the fanciful pets that roam in our garden. Meanwhile, I began to plan the interiors, striving for a fusion between Moroccan bohemian luxe and intrepid global nomad. My weekends were spent in the souks, haggling with carpet dealers, negotiating with potters, and chatting with woodworkers. I became an ardent student of Moroccan decor, my appetite insatiable for information on dyes and finishes, patterns and furnishings, and so much more. I began sharing what I was learning on my blog with a growing group of eager design fans.

Moroccan style is attainable yet exotic, practical yet mysterious, and a little splash of it goes a long, long way.

Four years later, Peacock Pavilions is built, its walls painted, its floors tiled, its gardens planted. Moroccan rugs have been unfurled on the floors, the colors ranging from elegant ivories and dramatic blacks to enticing saffrons. There are cozy banquettes piled high with embroidered cushions and tea tables made from hand-etched trays. Lanterns hang in clusters from the ceilings, casting intricate patterns onto the floors below. Collections of Moroccan pottery—in shades of turquoise and jade—gleam from every corner. And bookcases are home not only to books, but to all manner of intriguing objects from the souks.

Peacock Pavilions is a home I could never have dreamed of in a style I could never have imagined for myself when I was living in the United States, like the house in a tale of a kingdom far, far away. And yet it is quite astonishingly mine. But no matter where you are—whether in Manhattan or Sydney, Los Angeles or London, Dallas or Paris, or anywhere else—Moroccan style can be yours, too. It is attainable yet exotic, practical yet mysterious, and a little splash of it goes a long, long way. So come along with me on a journey into the pigmented and patterned world that is Moroccan design.

MOROCCAN GREETINGS

Greetings are very important in Morocco, and they are elaborate. Even if you see the same people every day, hellos may involve multiple cheek kisses, shakes of the hand, pats on the heart, inquiries about health and family, and poetic wishes of good tidings.

SALAMU ALAYKUM	Hello (literally, Peace be with you)
ALAYKUM SALAM	Hello to you, too (response)
SABAH AL KHEIR	Good morning
SABAH AL NOOR	A light-filled morning to you!
SABAH AL WARD	A morning filled with flowers to you!

MEES AL KHEIR	Good afternoon

KIDAYIR[A]? LA BESS?	How are you doing? Fine?
LA BESS	Fine (response)
KIDAYIR MA SAHAA? A'AILAH?	How is your health? Family?

BISLAMMA	Good-bye (literally, Go in peace)
TAALA FI RUSK	Watch your head (slang; Good-bye)
LALA SAIDA	Good night

An Introduction: Morocco and Moroccan Style

Thoughts of Morocco evoke images of *The Arabian Nights*: a kingdom filled with gold-domed palaces and high-walled casbahs (fortresses). A fantasy where beautiful harem girls lounge on cushions and genies emerge from bottles. A country where you can find witch doctors who mix love potions and snake charmers who charm cobras. A place where the air is always scented with orange blossoms and flying carpets substitute for taxis. Sounds like Morocco, right? Well, in an imaginary world, maybe. Although Morocco in reality is not quite the stuff of dreams and movies, it is no less inspiring, particularly when it comes to its design and decor. As for the snake charmers and genies? They really do exist—at least the former, anyway (and perhaps the latter, too!).

Morocco's cultural, linguistic, and design influences are extremely varied, in part because the country's location is so desirable that everyone has wanted Morocco for their very own. Over the years, Morocco has been conquered by groups of Arabs, Berbers and other Africans, Turks, and Europeans. Rome fought for four hundred years to keep control of the country, starting as early as 146 BC and continuing until the end of the third century AD. The Vandals and the Byzantines succeeded the Romans, and then Arab Muslims took control by the late seventh century (AD 683). And if that is not intriguing enough, Moroccan history is rife with tribal takeovers, plotting pashas, and banished kings.

Given its history, it is no wonder that Morocco is a polyglot nation. It boasts Arabic as its official language, Darija as its most widespread language, three Berber dialects with a strong showing, fluency in French, and a smattering of Spanish. In some ways, the most representative language is Darija, a distinctive Arabic dialect that is only spoken, not written; it is the fruit of its origins, with words begged, borrowed, or stolen from the tongues of Morocco's historical invaders—alongside the Arab, French, and Spanish imports, some Berber words have crept quietly into the Darija lexicon.

Magic also influences Moroccan culture and style in surprising ways. Moroccans believe in magic—the good and bad kinds alike. Belief in magic and the supernatural pervades the lives of Berbers in particular. Notions such as baraka (divine blessings and good luck), the evil eye, genies, and shur (sorcery), as well as powers associated with objects, substances, colors, numbers, and symbols, are not to be taken lightly. There is a reason why Moroccan doors are painted blue. There is a reason why carpets are covered with talismanic motifs and why henna designs flourish. In Morocco, protection against the evil eye and genies finds its way into decorative objects on a regular basis. From hand-shaped door knockers—a nod to the protective hand of Fatima, known as khamsa (five)—to the choice of fibers and substances that have baraka to the shiny metal sequins and pom-poms on textiles to ward off the evil eye and mischievous genies, magic is everywhere in Morocco.

Understanding Morocco's history and culture is essential to finding the answer to Morocco's design equation. So many foreign, indigenous, and religious influences have left their mark on Moroccan decor in indelible ways. And the end result is a heady mixture of old and new that has caught the design world by storm.

In the old cities of Morocco, there are architectural marvels to behold: palaces, fortresses, madrassas (Koranic schools), and riads (courtyard homes). Some of these are showpieces for sculpted plaster ceilings, mosaic tile walls, intricate carved woodwork, and marble fountains—all sublime remnants of yet more decorative eras. Old cities often rub shoulders with new cities built under colonial rule. These new cities are home to broad avenues, sidewalk gardens, stylish boutiques, and contemporary villas. A fusion of Moroccan design know-how and Western clean-lined sensibilities is noticeable in many of these areas.

But whether old or new, magical or not, Moroccan decor has one distinctive trait—a commitment to the handmade. In a world filled with factory production, shelves upon shelves of identical objects, and imports from China, Morocco offers another model: a place where things are made not by machine but by people. Centuries of artisanal tradition and expertise, thankfully, die hard. With their apprentices gathered around them, ma'allems and ma'allemas, or master craftsmen and craftswomen, can be found plying their trades in workshops around the country. Given the complexity of the work, it is not uncommon for apprentices to labor for years under their ma'allems, watching, learning, and doing small tasks before they are ever permitted to try their hand at making an object.

Moroccan workshops are often rudimentary places, sometimes with dim lighting and unfinished floors. All the more remarkable then that they are able to turn out things of such beauty. In metalworking ateliers, solder is melted over small flames. Craftsmen use the smallest of saws to cut minute designs out of brass, or employ a chisel and a hammer to pierce lanterns with delicate patterns. In zellij (enameled tilework) workshops, apprentices draw lines onto the backs of tiles so that ma'allems can cut them with precise blows of a chisel. The myriad small, fashioned furmehs (tiles) are arranged into awe-inspiring mosaics. In homes or cooperatives, women hand-knot pile carpets, tamping down each yarn with a heavy wool comb. Meanwhile, artisans methodically weave strands of sabra (cactus silk) on large looms and make bushy pom-poms with a snip of a scissors and a wrap of some yarn. In leather workshops, men wielding large shears cut skins into shaped panels. These panels are carefully sewn together to make ottomans or poufs. In woodworking ateliers, craftsmen patiently hand-carve calligraphy or floral designs into plain pieces of wood. These become focal points for banquettes (custom-made couches). In geps (carved plaster) workshops, men covered in

> Whether old or new, magical or not, Moroccan decor has one distinctive trait—a commitment to the handmade.

white powder make plaster friezes and medallions. Each of these plaster creations is fine-tuned by hand in the client's home, the joints blended seamlessly. And the list goes on. Everywhere, every day, Moroccan artisans are creating decorative objects, one by one, each by hand.

This blending of centuries and influences, as well as artisanal traditions, has led to a distinctive Moroccan style that has become iconic. Given its complexities, Moroccan design is not for the minimalist but for the modern-day maximalist. But that does not mean cluttered decorating. Rather, it means layered decorating—similar to a school textbook with translucent pages that overlap until the full image becomes clear. Ultimately, Moroccan style is a scintillating combination of strong architectural shapes; sublime decorative finishes; vivid, inky colors; intricate, fresh patterns; and one-of-a-kind objects.

In Part I of this book, you will find chapters dedicated to Moroccan architecture, finishes, colors, and patterns. These chapters are intended to provide you with the basic building blocks of Moroccan design so that you can apply ideas in your own home with ease. Of course, these design principles can be interpreted in many different ways depending on the nature of your space. Thus, in Part II of the book, there are specific chapters on Moroccan living and dining areas, bedrooms, kitchens and baths, and outdoor spaces and gardens. These chapters are meant to be inspirational, encouraging you to rethink, revamp, or redesign particular areas in your own home to add elements of Moroccan style. "Bringing It Home" boxes scattered throughout the book give you practical suggestions to help fast-track Moroccan design and decorating concepts, whether you live in a tiny apartment, a big house, or somewhere in between. Several fun how-to Moroccan decorating projects are provided to urge you to roll up your sleeves and do it yourself!

In Part III, the book's conclusion, there is a chapter on key Moroccan furnishings and decorative objects, as well as a chapter on shopping and design resources. These chapters are meant to provide suggestions about what things to buy, as well as information about where to buy them. Additionally, there are recommendations for specialists and suppliers who are experts in Moroccan design, so that you can continue your Moroccan decorating journey long after you have turned the book's last page.

THE EVIL EYE AND GENIES

Mentioned in the hadith (the words and deeds of the Prophet Muhammad), the evil eye can be described as a glance combined with a compliment. Compliments are believed to be dangerous if they are associated with envy and coveting; a person's good fortune, good health, or good looks may provoke envious people to cast the evil eye. The evil eye is believed to have the potential to cause harm to the object of envy, such as one's healthy baby, new car, fine job, or happy marriage. Some Moroccans believe that if not thwarted, the evil eye can provoke sickness or misfortune, and thus every effort must be made to circumvent it through the use of symbols, substances, and talismans. The evil eye is not just a Muslim superstition; the idea that a malicious and envious glance has the power to harm is a near-universal concept that dates back to the beginning of human civilization. The first written record of the evil eye is said to be from more than five thousand years ago. The King James Version of the Bible also warns of the evil eye in both the Old and New Testaments (Deuteronomy 28:54; Proverbs 23:6; Luke 11:34).

Many Moroccans (and, more generally, many Muslims) also believe in supernatural spirits, mentioned in the Koran. In Arabic, these spirits are called *jinni* (singular) or *jinn* (plural); in Darija, they are identified as *jinn* (singular) and *jnun* (plural). In the West, they are often referred to as *genies*. According to the Koran, God created three types of beings: angels, humans, and genies. Genies—who possess free will and can be either good or evil—are said to have been created from fire or smoke. Satan is thought to be a genie who rebelled against God. Although belief in genies is present throughout the Muslim world, these beings are an especially common theme in Moroccan tradition, folklore, and belief. Accordingly, Moroccan homes use prayers, as well as particular objects and substances, to appease them.

SNAKE CHARMERS

The presence of snake charmers on Marrakesh's famed Jemaa El Fna is as sure as the imam's call to prayer from the nearby Koutoubia mosque. With their ghaitas (Moroccan folk oboes) and their wooden crates, the men of the Aissaoua brotherhood slowly set up their stations each day on the square, as their fathers did before them. From out of the crates, they pull the slippery coils of cobras and vipers, pythons and rat snakes—celebrity tourists from Morocco's southern Guelmim-es Semara region.

With the shrill sound of the ghaita, the snakes come to life, "charmed" by the oboe's tune (or merely provoked by the charmers' incessant prodding and much unwanted attention). If myth is to be believed, the men of the Aissaoua brotherhood are immune to snake venom, giving them the perfect credentials for snake charming. Or is it that they merely remove the creatures' poisonous venom glands? The truth remains a mystery, and that's part of the fun.

A vintage Moroccan poster is a riff
on my life in Marrakesh. ⨍

PART I

Discovering Moroccan Style

Morocco's history and design influences have led to an architectural style that is mysterious and exciting. To live in Moroccan style means to live in a world that is not easily apparent to the outside eye. If you are lucky enough to penetrate beyond the heavy front doors of an upscale Moroccan home, private sanctuaries of beauty filled with courtyards, domes, arches, and fountains await you. Surfaces are richly decorated, patterns abound, and color is everywhere. The result? A delicious recipe for creating a memorable home. But before you dive in and paint your home in shades of deep red or cover your surfaces with complex designs, read on. In the following pages you will find a design primer on the fundamentals of Moroccan architecture, decorative finishes, colors, and patterns and learn about the different design influences that have made Morocco a melting pot of inspiration worldwide.

chapter 1

EXPLORING ARCHITECTURE

Moroccan architecture is the sublime product of the country's history and the result of many different design influences. Morocco has always been coveted, and it has survived centuries of conflict, conquest, and land grabs. Each of the invaders left a lingering mark on the architectural landscape. And so it is that the Morocco of today is the consequence of its complex past—a beautiful (if blood-spattered) architectural and design story.

Fortresslike Architecture

Because of its strategic location on African and European trade routes, Morocco has frequently been fought over. Indeed, over the years, the country has been controlled by different groups of Africans, Arabs, Europeans, and Turks. When a place is constantly under attack, security becomes a top consideration, and Moroccan architecture emerged as one that was essentially defensive in nature. It is no wonder that high, thick walls surround the medinas (old cities). Entry through medina walls was only through guarded, tall, fortified doors in locations where comings and goings could be carefully monitored. And within the city walls, dars (houses) also were built like burly bouncers, with blank exteriors and few entrances or windows. Today, most dars remain mysterious, with the exteriors revealing little of what lies inside.

Below: The exterior of the two-story pavilion at Marrakesh's Menara Gardens is plainly decorated, giving little indication of what lies within. Opposite: A fountain is decorated in Moroccan mosaic tile, known as zellij.

External Influences

Moroccan architecture is a blend of many different design influences: Islamic, Spanish, and French, to name just a few. Each of these outside influences left a design imprint on Morocco, which the country modified and made its very own.

ISLAMIC INFLUENCES

The Islamic world has an awe-inspiring tradition of architecture and design that is refined, elegant, and precise. All the characteristics of Islamic architecture are on display in mosques, palaces, and tombs throughout the Islamic world, setting the trend for many other buildings and showcasing some of the most impressive structures and patterns ever created.

Not surprisingly, Morocco was not immune to Islamic architectural beauty. The country was too far away from the centers of the Islamic empire to be under its direct political (or architectural) control. In fact, al-Maghrib, the Arabic name for Morocco, means "westernmost," showing just how very distant the country was. Nonetheless, Morocco's conversion to Islam brought with it many new architectural ideas that were adopted and adapted (and some say perfected) in its urban areas. Today, Islamic design influences can be seen in Morocco's use of tiles and fountains, the incorporation of geometric and floral patterns, and the existence of a multitude of impressive mosques.

Tiling: Moroccan tile was influenced by Persian tile, which originally came to Morocco via the Arabs and soon became a popular way to make surfaces attractive. While Persian tile was traditionally blue and white, green Roman tile also played a role in Morocco's love affair with colored tile. However, as with all things, Morocco took the tiling concept and coloring and changed it, which means Moroccan tile can now be

found in a huge range of colors—Morocco is the only place in the Arab world to have so much variety.

Fountains: Centuries ago, before Islam arrived in Morocco, water was already important, given the desert climate and the folk traditions that used water to treat illnesses. Under the country's Islamic conversion, water became yet more central. Thought to be a gift from God, water is a symbol of paradise in Islam, and Islamic rules also mandate cleanliness before prayer. Accordingly, public fountains were built in abundance to ensure that clean water was readily available for everyone. Ornamental grillwork was used to help keep fountain water clean, and fountains became more and more decorative. Stunning fountains can still be seen in public buildings and private homes throughout the country.

Geometric and floral design: Islam does not encourage the portrayal of human and animal figures. In fact, a stern Islamic hadith recorded by Ibn Hanbal says, "Painters will be among those whom God will punish most severely on the Judgment Day for imitating creation." As a result, tastir (geometric) and tawriq (floral) patterns emerged prominently in Morocco. The arabesque (repeating geometric pattern) symbolizes eternity and is said to prompt meditation on the eternal nature of God. Both tastir and tawriq patterns can now be found everywhere in Morocco on tile, wood, stucco, and most other materials and surfaces.

Mosques: With Morocco's Islamic conversion came the building of mosques. By some accounts, Morocco has as many as 3,500 mosques today, many quite striking. However, even with buildings of such a religious nature, Morocco managed to tweak the original architecture. Unlike in other countries, the aisles in Moroccan mosques are perpendicular to the qibla wall. (Qibla is the direction in which Muslims must pray, facing toward Mecca, in Saudi Arabia.)

Opposite: Marrakesh's Koutoubia Mosque stands like a beacon outside the old city walls, acting as a meeting point for travelers from around the world. Left: An elaborate Moroccan fountain features geometric (tastir) and floral (tawriq) patterns in mosaic tile and lacy plaster, creating a most decorative spot to wash hands. Above: Different mosaic tile patterns work themselves from the floor up the wall—proof positive that patterns can be happily mixed and matched.

SPANISH INFLUENCES

Spain, particularly southern Spain, has much in common with Morocco. Not only is the climate similar, but both countries share a love for decorative detail and a passion for exuberant color. So it comes as no shock that Moroccan design has been significantly influenced by its neighbor to the north. Refugees fleeing from fallen Muslim Andalusia in the south of Spain in the 1500s brought a number of architectural and design ideas with them across the water to Morocco. Today, Spain's design influence can be seen in Morocco's roof tiling, its numerous cusped and horseshoe arches, and its Andalusian-style gardens.

Overlapping roof tiles: Handmade and hand-glazed, overlapping roof tiles—like jewelry for the roof—are a Spanish tradition that was adopted in Morocco and elsewhere. In some parts of the country, especially the northern areas closest to Spain, such as Tangier, these roof tiles are particularly common. Roof tiling helps define and harmonize Morocco's urban landscape in a distinctly Spanish way.

Cusped and horseshoe arches: Many of the arches seen in Moroccan buildings and homes came via Spain. Cusped arches are made up of a number of foils (rounded indentations), giving a cloverlike shape to the arch. Horseshoe arches are shaped like a keyhole and can be rounded, pointed, or lobed; the horseshoe arch is so distinctive in Moroccan and Spanish architecture that it's also called the Moorish arch.

Andalusian gardens: Spain's Andalusian gardens are some of the most famous in the world, with the garden of the Alhambra in Grenada being one of the grandest. These particular gardens have been the design inspiration for numerous Moroccan gardens. Their influence can still be seen today, in terms of both landscaping and hardscaping, in Morocco's public and private gardens alike.

Right: These huge keyhole double doors in the Marrakesh medina are a shining example of Moroccan ornamentation. Made entirely of hammered brass, they catch not only the light but also admiring glances from passersby. Patterned tile with a decorative border topped by sculpted geps work surrounds the doors. It's no wonder that the turbaned owner of the shop next door smiles so broadly. Following pages: In Sylvain's three-story Essaouira riad, varied cement-tile patterns in similar colorways meld seamlessly and help create graphic texture. Furnishings are kept deliberately minimal to show off the riad's architecture.

FRENCH INFLUENCES

In the late 1800s and early 1900s, before the French protectorate was established in 1912, real estate speculators in Morocco were building left, right, and center, hoping to turn a profit. The chaotic, rushed building meant that Moroccan cities were becoming increasingly disorganized, with little urban zoning and muddled city centers that included crumbling shacks next to opulent five-story houses. Under the protectorate, French architectural standards helped to establish and maintain control, while at the same time respecting Morocco's architecture, traditions, and culture.

In an effort to preserve and protect Morocco's "Oriental charm" and promote tourism, the French made rules for new construction in the medinas. These regulations were primarily based on preexisting (although not strictly adhered to) Moroccan architectural and cultural principles:

- Buildings are not to exceed four stories in height.
- Twenty percent of a building's area must be dedicated to a courtyard or a garden.
- Balconies may not overlook neighboring courtyards.
- Doors may not face each other across a street (to protect privacy).
- Roofs must be flat.

The French also built new, European-style cities on the outskirts of the medinas. In a quest for responsible, controlled urbanism, a government overseer was appointed to develop each of the major cities. There was to be a central urban area, along with designated districts for commerce, administration, industry, homes of the elite, and homes of blue-collar workers. Everything and everyone was to be organized and to have its place.

In Casablanca, this model was implemented fairly rigidly, but cities like Marrakesh (with smaller European populations) escaped such regimented planning. Nevertheless, French architectural inspiration was felt in big cities and small cities alike. The French influence also was demonstrated in the new public parks and wide radial streets—a significant contrast to the private courtyard gardens and twisty alleys of the medina. These new city boulevards and streets were lined with buildings that followed specific rules, including uniform height and arcades in front. The French also used the new cities in Morocco to experiment with modernism and other movements, like art deco.

Similar to public spaces, European private villas had to follow architectural and landscaping guidelines, although there was more flexibility than in the medina. Many French homes incorporated Moroccan architectural elements, like mashrabiyas (lacy dowel-work screens), ornate tiling, horseshoe arches, and so on.

La Mamounia Hotel is one of Morocco's historical treasures. It is named after its two-hundred-year-old gardens, which were given as a wedding gift to Prince Moulay Mamoun by his father. The hotel itself was designed in 1923, by the French architects Henri Prost and Antoine Marchisio, who fused traditional Moroccan designs with the popular Art Deco look of the 1920s. A recent complete renovation of the hotel has been led by the French designer Jacques Garcia. Inlaid marble floors, zellij-covered columns, and oversized lanterns create an unforgettable ambiance.

It's all sinuous lines in pure white on the rooftop terrace of *Avel Mor* (which means "the wind of the sea" in Breton), an old three-story Essaouira riad owned by Parisian lawyer Catherine Charpentier. The blue railing faces the riad's central courtyard, flooding it with light on sunny days. The blue is echoed on the riad's arched doors.

Moroccan Architecture Today

Moroccan architecture today remains very much a combination of the old and the new. In the medinas, courtyard houses, hundreds of years old, nestle close to one another. Although many of these homes have been modernized, freshened, and refurbished, their architectural bones remain largely the same as when they were first built. Meanwhile, in the new cities and suburbs, villas boast air-conditioning, the latest appliances, and spacious rooms. However, many also include emblematic features, such as domes and arches, or architectural lines reminiscent of casbahs.

In Morocco, *dar* means "house." The word *riad* means "garden" but is used to describe a house that contains an inner courtyard garden. A *villa* is a large freestanding, upscale house in the new part of a city, built in the last 150 years or so.

THE DAR OR RIAD

Morocco's medinas step back in time. Because of their age—several centuries old—the medinas enclose mazelike networks of alleys and streets that contain homes, stores, and workshops. Walking through the narrow streets of a medina, there is little way to tell from the outside what a dar or a riad might look like on the inside. Families live in close proximity to their neighbors, with adjacent homes connected on three sides (the fourth side faces the street). Neighboring houses share a common exterior wall, which is plain, with few windows visible from the street and nondescript doors. In short, from the outside, most dars and riads have very little personality, and it is hard to distinguish between the houses of the rich, the middle class, and the poor. While Karl Marx might be pleased,

the lover of Moroccan decorative details might be a little disappointed.

However, medina houses are like gifts wrapped in brown paper. Because belying their plain-Jane exteriors, their interiors are often home to courtyards, gardens, fountains, and other enchanting surprises. And in marked contrast to the hubbub and commotion outside, the inside of a medina house is calm, cool, and collected, and it is often very beautiful.

The Marrakesh dar or riad is typically a one-, two-, or three-story house with a courtyard at its heart. Perhaps more than any other element, it is the courtyard that is the most singular architectural feature of homes in Morocco's medinas. Courtyards are not just lovely (although that might well be reason enough to warrant their existence)—they also serve several purposes. With the sky directly overhead, courtyards are said to provide access to God. In more mundane matters, courtyards also allow for private outdoor green space in the dense setting of the medina. In summer, planted riad courtyards capture cool breezes and supply shade and shelter from the hot sun. In winter, tiled courtyard floors absorb heat during the day and radiate the warmth to the rest of the house. Additionally, courtyards provide ventilation and let light into adjoining rooms.

The courtyard is almost always square or rectangular. In smaller houses, most courtyards are paved, with outdoor seating and potted plants. In larger riads, courtyards may include whole gardens with leafy trees and extensive plantings. Big or small, courtyard gardens involve plants that are attractive, edible, fragrant, or all three, providing a full sensory experience.

Natalie's tiled courtyard provides a cool
respite on Marrakesh summer days.

This Marrakesh courtyard is roomy enough for a
child to ride her bike within its perimeter.

Sometimes courtyard gardens are divided into four parterres (garden beds laid out in a formation and separated by paths) with fruit trees, roses, jasmine, or herbs planted in each quadrant; a marble or tiled fountain might be in the center. Water is a key element, and if a fountain is not at the courtyard's center, it is on one of the courtyard walls. Recently, a number of riad owners have taken to putting plunge pools in their courtyards as well.

The entrance to Moroccan medina houses is usually angled so that those at the door can't see immediately into the courtyard. The courtyard itself may be surrounded by a gallery or covered walkways, providing shelter from the sun and rain when one is walking from one room to the next—a very practical architectural element in houses that feature so much open-air living. The gallery is often an arcaded passage. Some houses don't have a gallery and feel a bit more contemporary and clean-lined.

On the ground floor, there is usually a small kitchen and two or more multipurpose rooms. The ground floor may also feature a bahou—a rectangular niche on the entrance wall in which a built-in couch is nestled. All ground-floor rooms open directly to the courtyard, blending indoor and outdoor spaces. Doors to the courtyard remain open most of the time, and sometimes there are no doors at all—only arched openings. The whole feeling is very welcoming and inviting, with a view of the sky straight up.

One or two narrow staircases lead from the ground floor to the second floor, where a few rooms will open to the covered gallery overlooking the courtyard. On the very top floor is the roof terrace, which can be treated as one or more outdoor rooms. Roofs are almost always enclosed by a parapet or low walls, originally meant to screen the women of the house from the prying eyes of curious neighbors. Accordingly, the roof terrace offers private areas for dining and for

Opposite, above: Adriano chose pearly white glazed bejmat tiles for the floors and courtyard pool of his Marrakesh riad. The patterned tiling on the walls gives the space a pleasing jolt of energy. Opposite, below: The courtyard of Marrakesh's Dar Rumi is a play in neutrals, with its graphic black and taupe checkerboard cement tiled floors. Color comes from the whole red roses floating in the oversized Moorish wall fountain. The fountain's arch is repeated on windows. Left: On Anne's riad mezzanine, the feel is decidedly modern. Clean-lined railings allow for an unencumbered view of the courtyard below. Floors made out of black dess (polished cement) gleam. Double doors and a wall are painted in shades of violet, the riad's leitmotif color.

lounging, napping, or sunbathing, as well as practical spaces to hang laundry to dry. Sometimes there is even an outdoor shower (perhaps the ultimate luxury in the middle of the city). Occasionally, there are stairs up to an even higher small vantage point. Over the roof terrace walls, there are views of the medina all around.

THE VILLA

Unlike houses in medinas, homes in new cities do not follow a particular architectural style. In addition to low-rise apartment buildings, houses pepper residential urban areas, surrounding suburbs, and the countryside. Large freestanding houses are usually referred to as villas. The term *villa* is a nod to Morocco's colonial past, evoking grand homes in faraway European cities. Not surprisingly, then, villas are not part of the traditional architectural vernacular, which revolves around the medina dar and riad. Rather, while villas draw inspiration from Moroccan architectural ideas, they are designed based on modern living needs.

Like dars and riads, villas tend to be private, hidden behind tall compound walls. This is in keeping with traditional Moroccan culture, where the home is a sanctuary for extended family and close friends, as Islamic traditions encourage privacy, in particular for women. Architecturally, villas are usually two or three stories tall. Public and private spaces are clearly delineated, with a premium placed on reception spaces. Some villas have interior courtyards, but not many, as there is often space for private gardens outside. However, lofty entry spaces—sometimes with little purpose—are designed to impress, and homes may have domed great rooms and soaring doors and windows. Typically, there are two or more living rooms with built-in seating, known as "Moroccan salons," allowing for ample room to entertain and seat guests. As is the case in riad-style homes, kitchens are less important and rarely of the open-plan variety, although "American-style kitchens" are increasingly in demand. Bedrooms and guest rooms may be located in a dedicated wing or in a separate guesthouse—there is a long tradition in Morocco and elsewhere in the Muslim world of friends and family staying for extended periods of time. Rooms in villas are more generously proportioned than those in riads, as room size is not dictated by an encroaching internal courtyard.

In some ways, Morocco's contemporary villas are designed with less thought to climate than those designed hundreds of years ago. (But in all fairness, there wasn't air-conditioning hundreds of years ago.) Most villas have many windows or sliding glass doors, even though glass is a poor insulator and electricity is expensive. Windows also tend to be larger and the walls thinner in villas than in medina houses, and so are less effective in dealing with the Moroccan heat. These are all compromises that homeowners are willing to make, however, in order to have lighter, airier houses than those found in the neighboring medina. The result is modern, light-filled havens of Moroccan luxury and charm. All the more for us to admire!

My architect husband designed an eight-sided dome with peepholes as a grand gesture in our great room. Lanterns shower down from the dome. A fountain filled with roses rests on the dess floor, which is tinted a warm tobacco color. Arched double doors with a chevron overlay lead out to the terrace.

PRACTICAL CONSIDERATIONS IN DAR AND RIAD ARCHITECTURE

Dars and riads are known for their unique architectural style. However, their beauty comes at a price, as they have a number of particular challenges.

- Because of the prime real estate devoted to courtyards, rooms in riads tend to be long and narrow. This can present some decorating constraints (and is one of the reasons that so many vintage Moroccan carpets are long and narrow, too).

- Ceilings are quite high (usually more than twelve feet high and sometimes substantially higher), calling for tall doors. Often double doors are divided horizontally or smaller doors are tucked into larger doors to make them less cumbersome to open.

- As there are very few windows on the outer walls of medina homes, the majority of natural light is provided via interior windows and open doors. Therefore rooms call for layers of lighting.

- Because of the high ceilings, thick walls, and open courtyard space, rooms can be quite chilly in winter, even with the doors and windows closed and heavy carpets rolled onto the floors. (On the plus side, this provides for a cool retreat in summer.)

- Kitchens tend to be small and cramped, and provide little storage. The eat-in kitchen is rare.

- Plumbing is often antiquated and problematic. Water pressure may also be unreliable.

Helmut's Marrakesh courtyard home is
unquestionably contemporary in feel.

chapter 2

UNDERSTANDING FEATURES AND FINISHES

Perhaps more than the buildings themselves, it is the architectural features and ornamental finishes that make Moroccan home design so intriguing. The variety of materials is impressive, from modest earth and plain straw to carved wood and chiseled marble. Architectural elements such as arches and domes, artfully shaped doors and windows, and fountains give houses a dramatic feel. Meanwhile, highly decorative finishes are frequently used for floors, walls, or ceilings, with arresting results. These are the sorts of characteristics that make Moroccan homes unique and different from their counterparts in the United States or Europe. In general, the humble mixes with the elegant, the plain with the ornate; and often the simplest materials are used in complex, intricate ways.

Basic Building Blocks

Construction materials may not be exciting, but they are the building blocks, quite literally, of all of our homes. Morocco has its own distinctive way of building—earthy and organic, particularly in the countryside. Basic building materials consist of earth, straw, lime, cement, brick, stone, stucco, tile, and wood. Traditional homes and perimeter walls—especially in villages and rural areas—are made out of pisé (rammed earth). Houses made of pisé appear to have emerged right from the ground, and indeed they have! Pisé can include straw and lime and may be surfaced with mud or stucco. A twist on this pisé eco-theme is that in some areas of Morocco—such as the Chichaoua region, Essaouira, and mountainous zones where good earth is in short supply—houses and walls are made almost entirely out of stacked stone, dug from the rocky terrain. These are truly feats of architectural precision, with stones exactly aligned with one another. That said, most modern urban construction is done with reinforced concrete, with other materials used primarily only decoratively. Given the country's arid climate, wood construction remains quite rare.

Right: Peacock Pavilions is made up of three reinforced concrete structures with hollow brick walls, and is surfaced in stucco. We chose the warm sand color for its seamless organic look in this desert oasis. Cement tiles in a matching color with plum borders are laid on a diagonal on rooftop terrace floors. Black wood trellises encourage jasmine and bougainvillea to climb toward the sky. Opposite: A series of lofty arches surrounds the central great space in the Peacock Pavilions guesthouse.

Architectural Features

Some of Morocco's most distinctive architectural features include arches and domes. These sweeping and memorable elements are the stuff of movies and are often what comes to mind when one thinks of Moroccan architecture. Less structural but no less distinctive are Moroccan doors, windows, mashrabiyas (turned wood screens), and fountains. Moroccan doors are so unusual and attractive that they are commonly recognized and sought after worldwide. While Moroccan windows are less elaborate than Moroccan doors, they also provide rooms with supplemental ornamentation and Moorish appeal. Unquestionably Islamic are the mashrabiyas found in older riads and dars. And in contrast to Western homes, fountains are incorporated into many interiors in new and old city homes alike.

ARCHES

Arches are ubiquitous in Morocco. Sculptural and feminine, arches can be found in public buildings and private homes, in big cities and small villages. In a marked departure from their angular counterparts in North America, arched doors, arched windows, and arched niches are commonly incorporated into Moroccan house design. Arcaded walkways, with their multiple arches, are also typical in larger medina homes, adding unmistakable architectural grandeur. Moreover, arches make their mark in smaller design features, whether carved on a wall in stucco relief, depicted in a mirror over a fireplace, or wound around the side of a table. The use of arches is seemingly endless and is sure to delight the eye.

There are a number of different types of arches, each with its own origins and meaning. The horseshoe arch, also known as the Moorish or keyhole arch, originated in Syria in the fourth century and then was refined in Spain. Because it is thought to repel the evil eye, the horseshoe arch shape is often used for exterior doors. The cusped and multifoiled arches (a cusped arch has fewer than five circular cutouts; a multifoiled arch has five or more circular cutouts) were originally developed by the Spanish Visigoths and were later used in European Romanesque architecture. The blind arch is one that is filled in or carved in relief, a nod to the prayer niche in a mosque and is used to add ornamentation.

Below, left: A blind arch on the dining room wall at Peacock Pavilions provides a clean-lined frame for an antique wall hanging. Below, right: A multifoiled arch acts as a decorative surround for a keyhole door on a side entrance of the Koutoubia Mosque in Marrakesh.

DOMES

The word for "dome" in Arabic is *qubba*, which means "shrine," perhaps because domes are often built as memorials or shrines to saints. But domes are also used as architectural features in many contemporary villas. Whether large or small, domes never fail to add glamour and drama. If a dome can be seen from the outside, it is structural. If it can only be seen from the inside, then it is likely to be purely ornamental—affixed to a flat ceiling, where it provides spectacular dimension.

Domes can be entirely smooth half globes, with or without the addition of glass peepholes. Ribbed domes, originally from the Middle East, are also common in

Morocco; the ribbing alternates positive and negative space and highlights the interaction between light and shadow. In addition to plain ribbed domes, there are star ribbed domes that have parallel ribs intersecting to form a star shape, invented in Spain and Iran in the tenth century.

Below, left: In the living room of Rose's Marrakesh villa, a round dome surfaced in ivory tadelakt (a lime finish) makes an airy statement. The Moorish fireplace provides an interesting focal point for the room. **Below, right:** *Peacock Pavilions' eight-petaled dome adds Moroccan flair to the skyline and can be enjoyed from up close on the rooftop terrace.*

DOORS

Doors are one of the loveliest and most unforgettable elements in Moroccan architecture, and the variety is truly remarkable. While front doors to villas are usually heavy and oversized, these same doors in medina homes are typically small and require stooping to enter. In general, front doors are solid, thick, and protective in nature. As for interior doors, in villas they are often standard sizes but may be arched, rather than rectangular, and bifurcated. In riads and dars, interior doors are frequently large, and they pivot to make opening and closing easier. Because of their size, double doors—rather than single doors—are common and sometimes split horizontally so that only the bottoms of the doors need to be opened. Alternatively, larger doors may enclose smaller doors, and only the latter will be used on a daily basis; these smaller doors require a step over the door base and a duck of the head, giving an *Alice in Wonderland*–like experience when entering and exiting rooms.

Moroccan doors can be extravagantly decorated. Exterior doors are often adorned with huge hinges or large metal studs, and interior doors are covered with detailed painting, often in tones of deep red and yellow, or carved with astral symbols and have painted highlights, as seen with more rustic Berber doors. The most ornate doors include gleaming etched-brass overlays or meticulous bone inlays. And even in the humblest village, doors are brightly painted in at least two colors and include curlicue metal detailing.

WINDOWS

In comparison to doors, windows play less of a starring role but may also be quite decorative. In medina houses, there are few external windows, in order to ensure privacy. However, these windows are often decorated with elaborate wrought-iron grilles that incorporate spiral and foliated motifs. Interior windows include clear or colored glass panes, the latter most often in shades of yellow, blue, and red. Colored glass windows typically open out from bedrooms to halls or walkways or are used in bathrooms for purposes of discretion. Like doors, windows are frequently made in arched shapes and are bifurcated from top to bottom. Unlike standard windows, chemmassiat—small windows made out of colored glass panes—soften the light but do not open or close; they are inserted directly into the plaster walls and are usually seen above doors.

Opposite, left: In Mary Charlotte's Marrakesh villa, an antique double door incorporates two smaller arched doors—a design that is not only beautiful but also useful for easy opening and closing. Opposite, right: An oversized door serves as the principal entry to Peacock Pavilions and includes an inset decorative floral plaque that we designed and cut ourselves. The door is so heavy that it rests on a wheel to make opening and closing it easier. The flanking closet doors are stenciled with a Moroccan pattern from Royal Design Studio. Left: In Catherine's riad in Essaouira, two turquoise arched windows with double panes let light from the courtyard into the small kitchen. A vintage Berber wedding chest with astral motifs provides a perch for flowers. The black and white checkered cement tiled floor adds a graphic punch.

A series of antique windows thrifted in the Marrakesh souks is featured in a guest room at Peacock Pavilions. They are hung from chains an inch or two from the walls so that their shadows can be admired in the afternoon light. The paint on the window shutters and frames was left in its original state for a casual charm. Originally, the ornate window grilles were meant not only to provide security but also to partially disguise women's faces as they peered outside. The cement floors are stenciled with a Moroccan design from Royal Design Studio. A hand-carved border adds tactile appeal to the simple wooden daybed.

MASHRABIYA

Characteristically Islamic, turned wood or dowel work, known as mashrabiya, is a stunning feature in some old Moroccan homes. At one time, mashrabiyas were built into the upper galleries, windows, balconies, and walkways of medina houses, as well as used in exterior windows. They served to conceal women from the curious eyes of male visitors while permitting women to see into the internal courtyard or street. Mashrabiyas also have the advantage of catching the light and casting lacy shadows across floors and walls. In addition to being used as built-in screening, mashrabiyas are often incorporated into banquettes and inset into cabinet doors.

Mashrabiyas are usually left unpainted, perhaps because their three-dimensional and intricate nature makes it difficult to get into all the dowel work's crevices. However, when painted, they may be found in shades of white, ivory, and the electric shade known as Majorelle blue. Alternatively, they are simply stained in a variety of wood tones.

FOUNTAINS

Fountains are undoubtedly one of Morocco's most sublime design elements and are frequently integrated into home interiors. They are most often seen as the centerpieces of living rooms or salons but are also found in entryways or foyers, to greet guests. Fountains come in many varieties, ranging from simple to elaborate. In addition to freestanding fountains, wall-mounted versions are common. They may be tall or knee-high with spouts trickling water into one or more receptacles. Fountains may also be simple, uncomplicated basins set into floors with small spouts at the center. Because of Islamic strictures, fountains are never figurative in nature.

Fountains are typically carved out of marble or made of cement. Sometimes the surface is covered in tadelakt, a burnished lime finish that is water-resistant. The most visually spectacular (and most archetypal) fountains are entirely covered with mosaic zellij tile in two or more contrasting colors. (See page 102 for more about zellij.) Occasionally, twenty-four-pointed star patterns are found on zellij fountains; the effect is extravagant and dazzling. In homes, fountains usually come in flower shapes or in modern square and round forms. Octagonal fountains also are not uncommon, symbolic of the eightfold nature of the Islamic paradise. Traditionally, the water in fountains is sprinkled with rose petals or whole roses, a beautiful addition to any space.

Opposite: For a bedroom in his Marrakesh riad, Helmut commissioned a sophisticated version of mashrabiya. The delicately carved patterns filter the light and cast intriguing shadows. The huge panels can be rolled open to allow a view into the courtyard and let in yet more light. Above: A marble triple-tiered fountain, hand carved with Arabic calligraphy, adds unmistakable glamour to Marrakesh's Tanjia restaurant, particularly when filled with whole red roses. The sound of the trickling water also provides a cool sense of serenity to all those who linger. Left: In lieu of a fountain in her Marrakesh villa, Stephanie floats flowers in an oversized bowl. It's a lovely Moroccan touch at a fraction of the price.

Decorative Finishes

Morocco is famous for its decorative finishes, and there are specific applications for specific surfaces. Floors, walls, and ceilings all get special attention and their own treatments.

FLOORS

Floors play an important decorative role in Moroccan homes, particularly on the ground floor and in public spaces. Wall-to-wall carpeting is rare, and wood is infrequently used for flooring because of its scarcity in Morocco's climate. Instead, floors are most often found finished in dess (polished cement) and tile.

Dess

Dess is a popular flooring method in Morocco, especially for outdoor spaces but increasingly for indoor spaces as well. Although dess literally means "bare ground," traditional dess was actually a combination of 75 percent earth and 25 percent lime. This mixture was hand-hammered with heavy mallets until it became hard and slick. Given how labor-intensive this process is, dess now simply refers to a thin coating (approximately ⅜ to ⅝ inches [1 to 1.5 cm] thick) of smoothed cement mixed with a small quantity of lime that is applied to a concrete slab floor—a reasonable facsimile with a similar effect. The smoothed cement may be tinted in numerous colors and is a simple, cost-effective way to give floors personality. It's also possible to apply superficial patterns to dess floors for ornamental appeal. While generally hard-wearing, smooth cement floors are prone to cracking; seams or plastic joints are often added to reduce this possibility.

For the outside terrace of their Marrakesh villa, Geraldine and David used black dess in combination with bejmat tile. It's a glamorous and striking look.

Tile

Moroccan tile is a fantastic option for flooring, with subtly or boldly tiled surfaces showing up in every room of the house. Common floor tiles include bejmat and cement tile.

Bejmat tile: Bejmats are handmade clay rectangular or square floor tiles. Traditionally, bejmat tiles were used for patios and courtyards, but they are now also seen in interior rooms. Historically, bejmats were glazed in white, green, or blue but now can be found in a wide range of colors. Bejmats are often laid in a two-color herringbone pattern, most frequently green and white, or blue and white; it is a look that is graphic and modern, although it has been around for hundreds of years. Additionally, many homeowners prefer to leave their bejmat tiles unglazed or put a clear glaze or wax on them for a subtle effect.

Cement tile: Cement tile may be found in many patterns—from traditional to ultramodern—and the color variety is phenomenal. Tiles usually come in eight-inch squares but may also be found in four-inch sizes, as well as four-inch-tall plinths. Cement tiles have a hand-finished, imperfect appearance, with tints that are chalky or inky and generally not uniform. Some hues are prone to fading in sunlight, and the tile does scuff easily (particularly dark colors). Cement tiles are also porous, so they must be sealed (and even then they might stain). However, for the most part, cement tiles are sturdy and relatively inexpensive. They are particularly good for warm-weather climates, as their surface stays cool and yet they are soft to the touch.

Sunny yellow cement tile from Popham Design livens up a bathroom at Peacock Pavilions.

decorative floor surfaces

- **SPLURGE ON GLAZED BEJMAT TILES** for a hallway or a bathroom. They gleam in the light and add a "wow" effect.

- **INSTALL UNGLAZED BUT TREATED BEJMAT TILES** around a pool or on patios and decks. This organic look blends seamlessly with landscaping.

- **CREATE A TILE CARPET** by combining borders and patterns. This is especially good for families with pets who find carpets to be too high maintenance.

- **USE CEMENT TILES** as flooring in basements, which may be prone to leaks or flooding. Consider a graphic tile to upgrade the look and feel.

how to

INSTALL A MOROCCAN CEMENT TILE FLOOR

A Moroccan cement tile floor is sure to add pizzazz to any room and is ideal for spaces where a carpet is not recommended, such as kitchens or bathrooms. Along with paint, this is one of the quickest ways to completely change the ambiance of your room.

MATERIALS

- Level
- Cement tiles
- Thin-set mortar
- Tub for water
- Trowel and/or wire brush
- Sponge
- Sealant
- Grout
- Scotch-Brite pads or fine-grained water sandpaper

PREPARATION

- Ensure that the surface to be tiled is level, clean, and perfectly dry.

- Mix up the tiles from several different boxes, since nuanced color variations are inherent in the manufacturing of tiles.

- Submerge the tiles in clean water to remove any dust from the backs before installing.

DIRECTIONS

1. Install cement tiles with thin-set mortar, using a double-adhesive process, whereby the mortar is applied to a clean, level surface and to the back of the tile using a trowel or a wire brush. During installation, press each tile gently into place by hand; never strike the tiles with a hammer (even a rubber mallet) as this will cause cracking. Take care to wipe down the surface of the tiles with a sponge immediately following placement to keep the mortar from setting in the tiles' porous surface.

2. Apply a sealant with a grout-release product immediately to the face of the tiles.

3. Let the tiles set for 24 hours before applying grout to the joints with a trowel or a sponge.

4. If any cement residue remains on the face of the tile, use a Scotch-Brite pad or fine-grained water sandpaper to gently remove the residue.

5. Once the tiles have dried, wash them with water and a mild soap to remove any chalky residue, which may appear as the tiles dry. Never use bleach or other acidic products on the tiles.

6. Leave the clean tiles to fully dry for about a week before the surface is used.

NOTE: To enhance the color of the tiles after installation, apply a sealant or a traditional wax finish. The type and number of coats of sealant will have an impact on the look of the tiles, which naturally have a matte finish. Depending on the amount of foot traffic you have, the wax coat should be refreshed every few months for optimum effect.

WALLS

Walls in Moroccan riads feature layers of decoration and pattern. The lower part of the wall may incorporate a wide band of patterned cement tiles, glazed bejmats, or mosaic tiling known as zellij. (See page 102 for more information.) On the upper part of the wall, there may be a large swath of geps (carved, patterned plaster). Given the considerable expense involved in these kinds of applications, this sort of extensive decoration is rarely seen in newer villas. However, tadelakt, a special lime-based surface application, is increasingly popular for walls. Originally used as a waterproof surface treatment in hammams (steam baths), tadelakt may now be found on the walls of virtually any room in the house. Similar in effect to Venetian plaster, tadelakt keeps walls naturally dust-free and imparts a burnished glow.

Right: Helmut chose an unorthodox cantaloupe color for the zellij tile surrounding the arched doorway to his riad dining room. Ivory tadelakt gleams on the arch interiors and dining room walls. Black glazed bejmat tile, added to chair-rail height, and a black and ivory patterned cement tile floor complete the look. The colors are echoed in the room's oversized artwork. Opposite: In Dar Rumi, walls are a taupe tadelakt, a perfect backdrop for the white central staircase with its polished black treads. The riad's patterned cement tiled flooring pulls the colors together and leaves a lasting impression. Oversized metal letters proclaim the owner's love for Persian poet Rumi, after whom the riad is named.

decorative wall surfaces

- **APPLY TADELAKT OR VENETIAN PLASTER** to the walls of your bedroom to create a moonlit glow. These are particularly good wall finishes for dimmer environments, as the burnished surface seems to emit light.

- **HANG A PIERCED LANTERN** from your ceiling so it casts patterns all over your walls. The look is dramatic and plays with patterns in a surprising way.

- **GO FOR A DRAMATIC FLOOR-TO-CEILING LOOK** with cement tiles in the bathroom. Alternatively, completely tile a shower stall in a graphic pattern.

- **MIMIC A RIAD WALL TREATMENT** by stenciling the lower third of your walls using a geometric Moroccan design. This also works well for a single accent wall, such as the wall a headboard is against.

GEPS (CARVED PLASTER)

There are few Moroccan decorative details more romantic than geps (or gyps), carved plasterwork. *Geps* comes from the word *gypsum*; when gypsum is mixed with water, it becomes plaster of Paris. Lacy, extravagant, and eye-catching, geps is typically used for upper walls, ceilings, tops of pillars, peaks, arches, or friezes. Ribbons of geps may also frame windows and doors. Geps is usually white, but multicolored versions do exist. Although seemingly fragile, geps is hard-wearing—some still survives from the twelfth century.

Geps may either be mixed on the spot and carved, or precast and further sculpted. If carved by hand, the plaster is applied and the motif is traced with a knife or made with a stencil. The artisan then chisels plaster away, leaving behind the three-dimensional pattern. Fine examples of geps have the plaster carved at different depths, giving it a dynamic effect. In recent years, premolded geps panels have grown more common, with prepared panels purchased from small plaster shops.

CEILINGS

In older houses, ceilings reflect the pinnacle of Moroccan craftsmanship and are the most elaborate surface in a room. Ceilings can be coffered and painted by hand. Alternatively, sculpted geps may cover the entire ceiling or be used to create ornate ceiling cornices. Some ceilings feature beautiful tataoui, painted or unpainted reeds that are laid out in geometric designs above or between ceiling beams. Other ceilings boast ornate zouak, the art of intricate painting on wood in geometric or floral patterns.

A ceiling in Marrakesh's Bahia Palace is a stunning example of decorative zouak ceiling work. Hand-painted floral and geometric patterns cover virtually every square inch, and the decoration overflows in layers onto the walls.

ceiling patterns

- **WALLPAPER YOUR CEILING** in a bold, high-contrast pattern. Keep the pattern large enough to make it eye-catching.

- **STENCIL YOUR CEILING** with a Moroccan pattern. (See chapter 10, Finding Decor and Expertise, for stencil information.) If it is too complicated, hire a professional to do it for you.

- **APPLY A MULTITUDE OF PLASTER MEDALLIONS** to the ceiling in a riff on geps. Keep the medallions identical for a clean look or vary them for a fun, modern appeal.

- **CRISSCROSS WOOD STRIPS** on your ceiling. The lattice pattern will pull the eyes upward.

chapter 3

CHARTING COLOR

Moroccans are addicted to saturated color and are not afraid of using it in generous doses. Neutrals are not espoused in the name of good taste. Rather, color is embraced as a source of happiness, visual stimulation, and beauty, a welcome juxtaposition to the sandy landscape in great swaths of the country. A love of color is as evident in tiny villages as it is in big cities. Color in Morocco has been a constant from ancient times until today.

In Moroccan homes, color starts with the front door. Doors are sometimes painted blue (for warding off the evil eye) or another brilliant shade, making every entry and exit a memorable experience. And the color story does not stop at the door. Walls can be completely soaked in color, commonly in shades of soft sepia or ochre. Alternatively, tinted walls can be reserved for specific rooms, such as salons or bathrooms, where color is often used in inky abundance. Then again, striking color might be found in decorative tiled bands that run along the lower part of the walls. For floors, dess is dyed in gleaming multidimensional shades. Color combinations also make a graphic showing on the floor in dizzying patterned tiling. Even ceilings sometimes glimmer with opulent color, either with painted designs of deep reds, yellows, and greens or with colorful painted reeds nestled above the rafters in eye-catching geometric patterns.

Color is also used in high-spirited abundance in furnishings. Carpets in rich, dramatic shades—reds, pinks, and saffrons in particular—are thrown down on floors in every room in the house. In an Orientalist tour de force, banquettes often feature layers of textiles in sumptuous deep shades. Wood furniture, too, has surfaces painted in multiple hues, a surprising and lively touch. Tables are set with pottery in cheery blues, greens, reds, and yellows. Meanwhile, it comes as no surprise when several lanterns with multicolored panes are found dangling festively from ceilings.

And the fun continues out the back door to the garden or up the stairs to the roof terrace. Tiled tables in intricate patterns and bright hues are immune to the sun's rays. Pots drenched in Majorelle blue dot the landscape. Rattan garden furniture painted in joyful tints offers happy places to read or chat. Trellises and walls draped with flowering vines are living paintings in shades of yellow, pink, red, blue, and orange.

The whole Moroccan color effect is optimistic and exuberant or moody and glamorous, depending on the hues used. The color wheel is spun enthusiastically and often, a lesson in color theory that dates back as far as anyone can remember. In general, Moroccans tend to favor warm, rich colors, such as reds and ochres, rather than cold, pale hues, such as light pinks or soft greens. They also are fond of bright, sunny colors—for example, vivid yellows or electric blues—as opposed to pastels of any hue. While long expanses of a single color are common, colors are often mixed in pairs to form patterns. A single shade may be matched with white, as a graphic counterpoint; historic color combinations include green and white and blue and white, the color duos often found in floor tiling and pottery. Black is also frequently mixed in as an accent in small doses, such as in the fine striping at the end of many textiles. However, Moroccans do not limit themselves to two shades—riotous mixes of colors are not unusual, as evidenced in sabra throws, carpets, and mosaic zellij. Multiple colors in a single piece have a connotation of richness, each thread, dye, or paint having been purchased separately. In short, color is approached playfully in Moroccan design, to great effect.

In addition to matte colors, shimmery, reflective metallics, such as silver, gold, and copper, are in demand. These metallics are woven into textiles, stamped on leather, or used for flourishes on pottery; special surface treatments may add an extra luster and depth to color. The more shimmer, luster, and glow, the more desirable.

NATURAL AND SYNTHETIC DYES

Until the early 1900s, textile colors in Morocco were largely created from natural, plant-based dyes—from the vivid pink of the fuchsia plant to the bright green of wild mint. The color palettes varied by region and local flora, and often the way to make a specific dye was a well-guarded family secret. But prior to World War I, Europeans introduced synthetic dyes to the Moroccan marketplace, where they caught on quickly; they were inexpensive and quick and allowed for a greater range of color. Now both natural and synthetic dyes are available in Morocco. Natural dyes have an advantage over synthetic dyes, as they are colorfast. Synthetic colors sometimes run, requiring extra attention during washing, but they come in every color imaginable, including electric and neon shades.

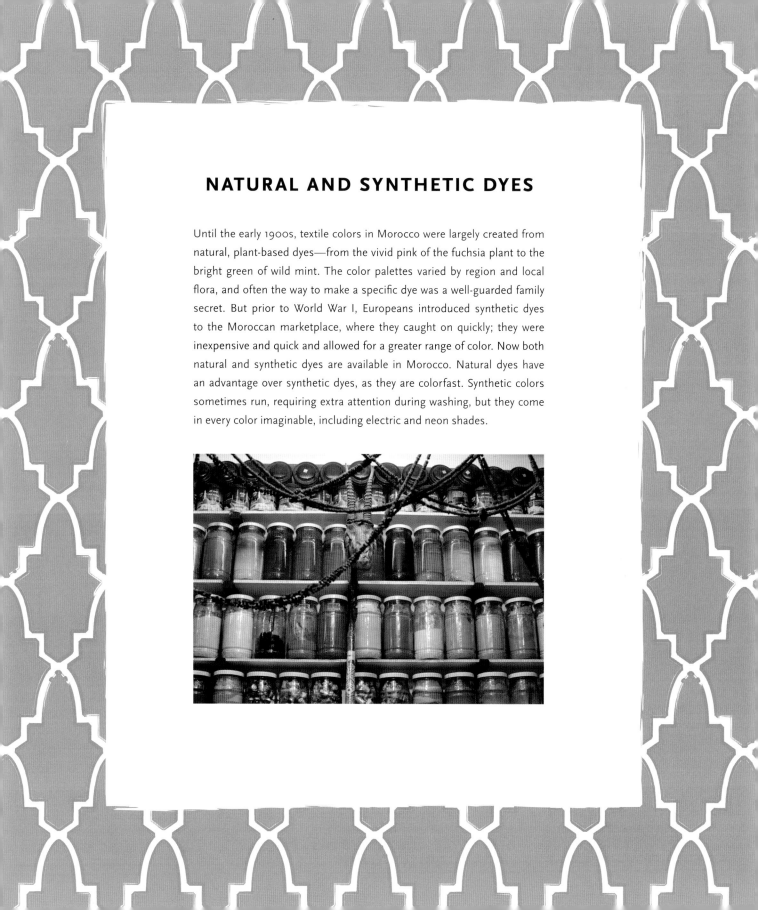

The Moroccan Color Palette

While the whole spectrum of colors is available when decorating in Moroccan style, certain colors have traditionally been more in demand; these include blues, reds, greens, yellows, oranges, whites, blacks, and beiges.

Right: Sacks of Moroccan pigments in brilliant shades are set out enticingly on the Essaouira sidewalk. Ladled out in large plastic scoops and purchased by weight, the pigments offer endless possibilities for tinting fabric, paint, and more. It's no wonder that it is hard for passersby to resist.

Opposite: My personal collection of handwoven Moroccan blankets is stacked up in "The Princess and the Pea" fashion. I've been collecting these blankets for years, seeking out shades of pink and rose, less common than reds in the Moroccan color spectrum. The blankets are entirely made of wool, cozy on chilly desert nights.

Blue

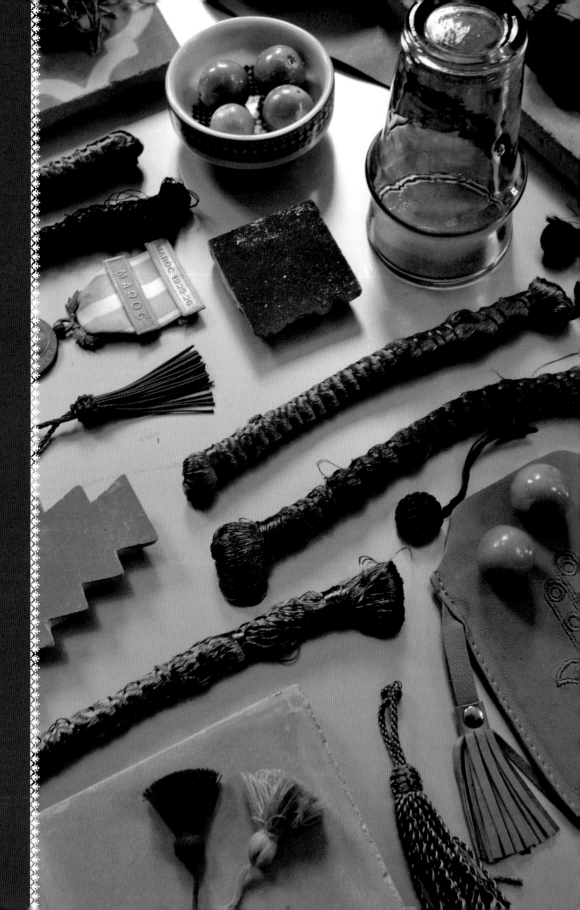

COLOR RANGE INCLUDES

- Greenish turquoise
- Fresh Fez blue
- Electric Majorelle blue
- Inky dark and light indigos

Use: Blue is associated with the city of Fez, as its namesake ceramics are made in intricate blue-and-white patterns. Indigo blue is linked to the western Sahara and Guelmim because of the distinctively blue turbans and dress of the Moroccan Tuareg people. Meanwhile, the psychedelic hue of Majorelle blue is often connected with Marrakesh. Blue frequently makes a showing in Moroccan tiling and thus is regularly found on floors and on the lower third of walls. Indigo is most often seen in textiles (but rarely in carpets, because of its expense). Majorelle blue is habitually used to paint garden pots and wicker garden furniture, as well as doors and window frames.

Symbolism: In Moroccan culture, blue is linked symbolically to the sky, heaven, and water, and the Berbers specifically associate blue with the sea. In Islamic countries, the color is thought to deflect the evil eye; for this reason, it is often used on doors or included in small pendants worn around the neck. Historically in Morocco, indigo—a major ingredient in blue dyes—was believed to have medicinal and cosmetic benefits. Some Berber women believe that indigo improves their complexions, conditioning the skin. Blue is linked to the planet Mercury in Morocco and elsewhere in the region.

Blue Dyes and Enamels

- Indigo (from the indigo plant, found in southern Morocco) is soaked in sulfuric acid and stabilized with alum to make dye.
- Majorelle blue cannot be made from natural dyes, only synthetic ones.
- Blue enamel can be made from imported cobalt.

NOTES: Indigo, particularly the darker version, is well known for standing up to sunlight. However, indigo items should be tested for colorfastness and should be washed separately.

1. INDIGO FABRICS
The striped sabra banquette in deep indigo blue holds up well in the intense Moroccan sun.

2. TADELAKT POTTERY
Use accents of blue pottery to create interesting focal points in a room.

3. TURQUOISE PAINT
Blue walls connect a room symbolically to the heavens.

Left: Majorelle blue, an electric shade of blue with violet undertones, was created by the French painter Jacques Majorelle (1886–1962), who was inspired by the color of a French worker's overalls. In 1924, Majorelle created the exquisite Majorelle Gardens in Marrakesh to house the world's most beautiful plants. Throughout this botanical paradise, he used the striking blue to paint the garden's fountains, pergolas, and pots. He also painted his Marrakesh house the vibrant hue, flouting the city's building restrictions. Years later, Yves Saint Laurent and Pierre Bergé, both admirers of Majorelle's creation, bought the garden and remodeled it. The scattering of Yves Saint Laurent's ashes in the garden after his death ensures that he will forever be associated with Majorelle's blue-tinted corner of Marrakesh. *Below:* Turquoise doors and windows and rattan furniture painted Majorelle blue adorn Catherine's riad rooftop in Essaouira.

White, Ivory, and Beige

COLOR RANGE INCLUDES

- True white

- Off-white/ivory

- Beige

Use: White is a favorite color of Moroccan Berbers, who are partial to the ivories or off-whites of undyed wools. Accordingly, this color spectrum is predominant in a number of popular Berber carpets, including those by the Beni Ourain and Marmoucha tribes. Many Berber blankets and capes are found in beige, decorated with fluffy pom-poms on the edges, or with sequins to add sparkle. Additionally, ivory is common in Moroccan haiks (fine long lengths of linen, wool, or cotton, previously used as clothing but now often made into bedding or curtains). Because of the heat, ivory canvas is frequently used to make tents for living or dining, tarps for shading on terraces, and covers for outdoor seating. Geps, the beautiful carved plasterwork, also is typically left white. White or ivory is regularly incorporated in Moroccan patterns as a counterbalance to darker, more striking colors in tiling, textiles, and pottery.

Symbolism: In Islam, white is a color infused with meaning, representing moral qualities. White connotes a fine character, a pure heart, and piety. Many Moroccan men wear white to the Friday prayers, and pilgrims to Mecca always wear white clothing. Moroccans believe a good-natured person has a "white" heart. White is also associated with cleanliness and good luck, as well as with beauty and femininity. White foods such as milk and eggs are prestigious and are often used in Moroccan magic to bring good fortune. In contrast, white is also linked to shrouds and mourning.

White Dyes and Enamels

- For ivories, no dye is necessary. The color is as found naturally in cottons and wools.
- Moroccans often leave ivory-colored textiles out in the sun to make them even whiter.
- White enamel can be made from zinc.

NOTES: In a number of recently made Berber carpets, bleach has been used to make beige carpets paler. Be aware that bleach renders wool fragile.

1. UNBLEACHED CANVAS
Use neutral shades on a rooftop; they blend in well with the surroundings.

2. WHITE CINDER BLOCK
Lacy patterned cinder blocks add an unexpected feminine touch.

3. NATURAL FOSSILS
A grouping of three neutral-colored fossils lends a textural effect.

Red

COLOR RANGE INCLUDES

- Salmon
- Rosy pink
- Fuchsia
- Apple red
- Brick red
- Carmine
- Bordeaux
- Violet

Use: Red is perhaps the color most associated with Morocco. Indeed, Marrakesh is known as the red city because of its salmon-pink-colored walls, which glow a richer color before nightfall. Houses in northern Morocco often feature red qermud (roof tiles). In terms of interior design, numerous carpets and flat weaves use red as a base. Unpatterned carmine-colored pottery is popular in upscale pottery shops—a fusion of Moroccan and European sensibilities.

Symbolism: In Morocco, red symbolizes female sexuality, fertility, and childbirth, in addition to happiness and marriage. The color is often connected with henna, which is thought to protect against the evil eye and contain divine blessings. The connection between the Moroccan royal family and the Prophet Muhammad is also symbolized by the color red. And as it is elsewhere, red is linked to the planet Mars.

Red Dyes and Enamels

- Red dyes made with madder root create a variety of shades, from orange to pale red, deep red, and purplish red. Color intensities depend on the amount of madder used and the temperature when boiling the dye. Carmine-colored dyes can be made from cochineal, a cactus insect that is dried. This produces a range of colors from scarlets to pinks. When mixed with salt, cochineal makes crimsons and oranges; when mixed with copper, it can also make different shades of violet.
- Dark red dyes are made from grapevine, too.
- Red enamel can be made from sand from Meknes, which is added to lead.

1. RED GLASSES
Red is a popular color for Moroccan glassware and pottery. It adds pop to everyday tableware.

2. PAINT IT RED
Red paint can be used in dramatic abundance for a Moroccan look. Try it in a hallway or a powder room.

3. USE FIERY COLORS
Red gives a Moroccan bang-for-the-buck when used in small saturated doses.

Black and Brown

COLOR RANGE INCLUDES

- Black
- Soft black
- Smoke
- Brown

Use: Black is a base color in Moroccan design and can be found in a wide range of items, including mosaic zellij patterns and carpets from the Tazenakht area. Original hand embroideries from the city of Fez often feature stark and intricate black designs. Black is also used as an accent color to add drama in Moroccan interiors. Depending on the material, true black is relatively rare; for example, in cement tile or in tadelakt surfaces, the color is almost always a very soft black or a smoke. Brown is found frequently in textiles, such as blankets, and in Berber tents, and is often woven from undyed goat or camel hair.

Symbolism: Although black is the color the Prophet Muhammad wore when he conquered Mecca, it often has negative connotations in Islam and the Arab world. Some think it is unlucky and connected with an inauspicious bird, the raven. Black also represents grief or something that is virulent and infectious. In Morocco, black is associated with the planet Saturn.

Black and Brown Dyes and Enamels

- Pomegranate peel is the key ingredient in natural black dyes. The peel is crushed and boiled and then the mixture is allowed to steep for days. Next, wool and indigo are added. Alternatively, vinegar is poured on iron shavings and mixed with powdered pomegranate peel. The more iron, the blacker the color; the less iron, the browner the color. Pomegranate peel can be replaced with pomegranate flowers to make the dye even blacker.
- Black and brown dyes are also made from dried figs that have been mixed with iron shavings or nails and left to sit for several days, or from cinnamon or henna.
- Black enamel can be made from Saharan pebbles.
- Brown enamel can be made from manganese.

NOTES: Because of their strength, natural black dyes can eat through fabric, which is why sometimes in older Moroccan textiles the color black is missing.

1. COMBINING TEXTURES
A black leather floor cushion coordinates perfectly with a black lacquer tea table.

2. BLACK TEXTILES
Adding a black sparkling pouf makes a statement and is easy on the wallet.

3. BLACK TADELAKT
Glowing black tadelakt walls give a cocoon-like feel to any room.

Green

COLOR RANGE INCLUDES

- Bottle green
- Blue green
- Grass green

Use: Green has a long history in Morocco. It is associated with the distinctive bottle-green pottery from the southern town of Tamegroute, located in the valley of the Draa River. It is one of the colors most frequently used in glazed bejmat tile (often paired with white in chevron patterns on the floors of grand houses) and in zouak painting on ceilings and furniture. Surprisingly, it is a hue that is seldom used in carpets and textiles.

Symbolism: Green is a color closely associated with Islam and with a heavenly paradise; there is a sura (a chapter of the Koran) that says that those in paradise will wear beautiful clothing of green (76:21). The Prophet Muhammad is purported to have loved green and to have worn a green turban and green robes. Some believe that green is the go-between that connects the red of hell and the blue of heaven. Others think that the fondness for green stems from the reverence desert Arabs hold for gardens and vegetation. Green is representative of fertility and symbolizes life, renewal, and growth. Green is also the shade of the Moroccan royal parasol and is found in the Moroccan flag. The color green is linked to the moon.

Green Dyes and Enamels

- Natural green dyes can be made from green walnut shells or from mint.
- Green dyes can also be made from mixing natural yellow and blue dyes together.
- Green enamel can be made from copper.

1. GREEN EMBROIDERY
Green tassels and embroidery are striking and accentuate any room accessory.

2. GRASSY GREEN
A saturated green door and the green in the patterned cement tile continue the grassy green trend.

3. GREEN WITH NEUTRALS
Shades of green can be just the right foil for beiges and creams.

Yellow and Orange

COLOR RANGE INCLUDES

- Gold
- Lemon yellow
- Dark yellow
- Orange yellow
- Orange

Use: Gold or metallic yellow is an important element in Moroccan design, threaded through textiles, embroidered on pillows, and stamped on leather home accessories. Plain yellow is frequently used in tilework, particularly glazed bejmat and zellij tile but cement tile as well. It is also incorporated into painted designs on doors and furniture. The color is perhaps most often seen in leather products, such as poufs and cushions, because the dye is particularly colorfast. Orange, too, makes a showing in leather items and is commonly seen in carpets.

Symbolism: Yellow represents the sun in Moroccan culture and is sometimes used in orb or almond shapes on the backs of capes for that purpose. Yellow also is associated with gold and spiritual wealth. The color is believed to be able to ward off evil.

Yellow and Orange Dyes and Enamels

- Larkspur, turmeric, spurge flax, and sumac are all used to make natural yellow dyes.
- Special pieces, including some old carpets from Tazenakht, occasionally use saffron as the key ingredient in yellow and orange dyes.
- A dye can also be made by adding takkoumt flowers and almond leaves to boiling water.
- Dyes are sometimes deepened by soaking fabric or leather in cow urine.
- Yellow enamel can be made from the rust from car radiators.
- Fez ore is also used to make yellow enamel.

1. GOLD METALLICS
Gold patterns should be used with an appropriately light touch.

2. YELLOW FURNITURE
Use yellow in outdoor furniture; the colors make for happy meals year-round.

3. SUNNY HUES
Shades of orange and gold up the ante on Moroccan textiles.

THE DYERS' SOUK

In every major Moroccan medina, one can find the dyers' souk, a place where fantastic shades of color mingle on a regular basis. Cotton hangs prominently around open squares, strung alongside wool in large undyed balls and sabra (vegetable silk from cactus plants), a more glimmering companion to its two thicker counterparts. It is in these dyers' souks that age-old techniques and dyes are used to turn wool, cotton, and sabra into a Technicolor dream coat of deep reds, indigo blues, and sunlike yellows. Using an ever-ready supply of wood, the dyers submerge the yarns or fabric of choice in a bath of water and dye; this is heated to 176°F (80°C). Vinegar and salt are added to the bath and the mixture is left, undisturbed, for thirty minutes. The salt and vinegar fix the color, preventing it from running during subsequent washes. Skeins and fabrics are left to dry before they are returned to their owners or sold in the souks.

Chunky skeins of pure wool yarn in delicious colors hang just waiting to be crafted into something beautiful.

incorporating color

- **PAINT YOUR FRONT DOOR** or one of your interior doors blue. Blue doors are common in Morocco; they're thought to ward off the evil eye.

- **ROLL OUT A RUG** in rich, variegated reds under your dining room table. It will stimulate your appetite and pump up the volume of the room. Red is perhaps the shade most commonly found in Moroccan rugs.

- **GO BOLD WITH COLOR** in your bathroom. Moroccans often opt for rich, saturated colors in their bathrooms and hammams, creating a deeply relaxing and mysterious environment.

- **LEARN FROM FRENCH PAINTER JACQUES MAJORELLE** and use Majorelle blue in your garden. Paint your pots and perhaps a trellis or two with this amazing shade.

how to

DYE A CONCRETE FLOOR

Dyeing floors is different from staining them. With dye, there is no chemical reaction with the concrete—it simply dyes the surface. Dyes can come in liquid form or as dry pigment, the latter to be mixed with a solvent (usually acetone). The color of the finished product and the depth that the dye penetrates into the concrete depends on the dye-to-solvent ratio. Dyes will not hide imperfections in the concrete; they are meant to enhance the variation that the concrete already has. Acetone dyes are made to be used on polished concrete floors that have not been sealed. If your floors have been sealed, the sealant will need to be removed before the dye is applied.

MATERIALS

- **Broom, vacuum, or mop**
- **Dye**
- **Solvent or water, as per directions on the dye**
- **Plastic bucket**
- **Rubber gloves**
- **Paint sprayer with acetone-safe plastic tips and seals**
- **Water**
- **Sponges**
- **Sealant (polyurethane or other)**

NOTE: When working with an acetone-based dye, make sure the room is well ventilated; open all windows and doors when dyeing floors. Wear protective gloves and glasses, too, as acetone dyes are highly flammable.

DIRECTIONS

1. Thoroughly clean the floor with a broom, vacuum, or mop. Let it dry completely before moving on to the next step.

2. Mix the dye in a plastic bucket according to the manufacturer's directions.

3. Wearing rubber gloves, load a paint sprayer.

4. Spray the dye onto the floor from a distance of about 2 feet (60 cm), using a circular motion.

5. The dye should penetrate the surface and be absorbed within about 1 minute. If working with a water-based dye, wipe away any excess with water and a sponge to avoid puddling on the surface.

6. Wait 15 minutes and apply a second coat, if desired, to darken the color.

7. Using the sprayer with a nozzle tip made for sealants, spray with a sealant. The dye dries quickly, so the floor can even be sealed the same day.

8. Let the sealant dry for several hours before using the floor. Dyed cement floors should be cleaned like any other floor—with a mild mix of soap and water.

chapter 4

UNCOVERING PATTERN

Moroccan style is not for the minimalist. In fact, visitors are often surprised by the extravagant use of patterns in older homes. It is not unusual to find different patterns on the floor, walls, ceiling, columns, doors, windows, and furnishings all in one room. It creates an astonishing and sometimes riotous effect! Surfaces are covered with multicolored mosaic tile, carved or painted patterned wood, and intricately sculpted plaster (or with all three!). Decorative applications are sometimes stacked like a layer cake, with floors blanketed with multicolored enameled bejmat tiles, lower walls boasting mosaic zellij tiles, upper walls

surfaced with sculpted plaster, and ceilings entirely patterned and painted. In addition, interior wood doors are painted with decorations or intricately carved, or both. Pillars in courtyards do not go neglected, incorporating mosaic tile treatments or including capitals made from sculpted plaster. Meanwhile, windows and second-floor balustrades encompass ornate wrought-iron grillwork. Patterned carpets are layered over patterned tile floors in a pattern-on-pattern montage. So, too, couches or banquettes in living rooms are covered with embroideries, patterned upholstery, and passementerie work, alongside multiple tea tables also elaborately painted with designs.

In short, in Morocco, pattern is to be embraced and adored, and the more the better. Lovers of the plain and simple might as well just go home.

Left: It's all about patterns in a guest room at Peacock Pavilions. I purchased the hand-carved Moroccan tea table in the Marrakesh souks. Our pink bougainvillea finds a home in a calligraphy-covered jug. The Moroccan patterned wall was a design commissioned from artist Melanie Royals and was executed by a team of American decorative painters. Opposite: Moroccan pattern makes an amazing showing on every surface in this little corner in Marrakesh. The pillar features meticulous white geps floral work. The walls are eye-catching with their intricate zellij mosaics. And if that is not enough, the heavy wood door in the background is hand carved with ornate geometric designs. The floor is patterned with cement tile laid on the diagonal.

Pattern Basics

There is a reason why there are no cupids flying among clouds or nymphs cavorting in the woods in Moroccan art. Following Morocco's Islamic conversion, art that depicted people and animals (whether portraits, statues, or other forms of representational art) was seen as competing with God's own perfect creations. Accordingly, figurative art was traded for geometric and floral motifs, and so it was that the intricate world of Islamic pattern came to Morocco. Some say that Islamic patterns are by their very nature democratic; as Islamic art rarely includes images of people, no race, color, or gender is ever left out. In this way, Moroccan art and pattern may be collectively identified with and its beauty appreciated universally.

Moroccan (and Islamic) patterns normally follow certain established styles: tastir (geometric patterns), tawriq (floral and foliage patterns), and calligraphy. Occasionally, these patterns are blended, creating fusions or layers of pattern. The same motifs are used in multiple media, whether in woodwork, tile, plaster, or embroidery.

GEOMETRIC PATTERNS

Tastir (Islamic geometric patterns) are hundreds of years old but still look fresh and modern. They are created by filling a space with straight-sided shapes. Basic shapes include the triangle, the square, the pentagon, and the hexagon. These elements are put together to form other shapes and motifs. Often elements are combined to form stars, which are an important motif in Moroccan geometric design. Indeed, many interlacing geometric patterns stem from a central star shape that emanates outward. Tastir patterns can include stars between eight and an incredible sixty-four points or even more. Certain stars are more common than others, and the most complex stars are usually only seen in palaces, mosques, and the grandest hotels.

In general, notions of symmetry and infinity are central to geometric patterns. This creates a rhythmic and trance-inducing effect, with patterns emerging from within patterns—an effect similar to optical illusions. Color is used to further emphasize specific patterns and symmetries, so that some patterns are more easily seen, creating contrasts. The simplest way to change the appearance of a pattern is to change its direction, rotate it, or replace colors or color combinations in order to focus on different aspects of the pattern. Each pattern repeats into infinity, interrupted only by the frame of the next architectural element.

Right: Guests leave their shoes at the door and don Moroccan slippers just about everywhere in Morocco. The slippers make an impression against this blue patterned tiled floor. Opposite, top: A tightly patterned red and ivory vintage flat weave features sequins woven in a sparkling grid design. Opposite, center: A selection of hand-excised tiles in geometric patterns and beautiful hues dazzles on a shop shelf. Opposite, bottom: Look at the sea of hand-cut blue and white zellij tiles long enough and the patterns appear to grow and change.

FLORAL PATTERNS

In Morocco (and in the Islamic world), floral and foliage patterns are known as tawriq. With their curved lines, these designs are much more fluid than the straight-edged tastir. They also tend to be less symmetrical and less regular. Nonetheless, balance and layout is still carefully considered in this style. Tawriq patterns may include many sorts of plant motifs, such as pinecones, leaves, buds, and small flowers, as well as vines. Tashjir (trees of life) are also regularly found in Morocco, with intertwining boughs, leaves, and fruits. Tawriq and tashjir patterns symbolize growth, life, and fertility.

Elaborate Moroccan tawriq patterns are found painted on wood panels (zouak); they are especially decorative when arranged to scroll across tea tables, doors, or entire ceilings. These floral patterns are also carved into geps, where their beauty is delicate and awe-inspiring. Additionally, tawriq patterns are excised into zellij or mosaic tile, where they mix with calligraphy as a decorative overlay, adding interest to intrigue. Tawriq designs are found much less often in mosaic zellij tile because of the difficulty in making small curved tiles by hand with a chisel.

Moroccan patterns enchant no matter the medium. They may be hand-painted in careful floral or geometric designs on tiles. On wood surfaces, these patterns are known as zouak. Meticulous designs may also be painstakingly cut out of brass and copper with a tiny saw. Alternatively, gorgeous patterns often make a showing in hand-carved geps. There is no end to Moroccan pattern use, just as there is no such thing as too much pattern.

CALLIGRAPHY

Beautifully executed written words are an art form throughout the Arab world, Morocco included. There are two major types of Islamic calligraphy seen in the Moroccan decorative arts: nashki, which is a rounded, cursive form of calligraphy, and kufic, which is more geometric in style. Letters are laid out horizontally, vertically, or in circles or other shapes. Frequently, floral tawriq motifs will be woven through the calligraphy, making it even more decorative (if somewhat harder to read). Moroccan calligraphy typically finds inspiration in the Koran or in the hadith, the words and deeds of the Prophet Muhammad.

Calligraphy is regularly used on walls, sometimes in the form of striking friezes above mosaic-clad lower walls. Often, calligraphy is excised into enameled tile: the tile is chiseled away, leaving behind the calligraphic writing in enamel. Calligraphy is also used in geps plasterwork or carved into wood. More recently, calligraphy or individual letters are painted by hand on pottery or printed on fabrics.

Below, left: The Arabic calligraphy panels that I have on my wall at Peacock Pavilions were made by my father in the 1970s and '80s. Below, right: Taking inspiration from the Moroccan habit of using calligraphy for interior design purposes, I commissioned a design from Melanie Royals for my office floor at Peacock Pavilions. But the patterns don't stop there. I also used Melanie's Moroccan patterns to stencil file folders and boxes in a crisp black and white. I made the shelves myself using decorative Moroccan cinder blocks. This idea is easy to replicate anywhere.

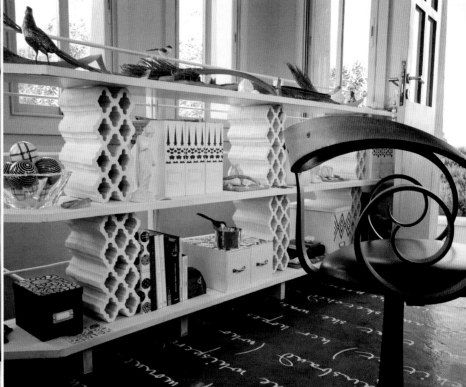

moroccan pattern

- **STENCIL A DOOR** with a geometric pattern. Or consider stenciling an entire floor to completely change the look and feel of the room. (See chapter 10, Finding Decor and Expertise, page 234.)

- **LAY DOWN PATTERNED CEMENT TILE** for a burst of geometric or floral goodness. This works well even in small doses, such as in entryways or bathrooms.

- **UPHOLSTER A SIDE CHAIR** with a Moroccan-inspired fabric with a geometric pattern. Or use the fabric to make throw pillows for your couch or bed.

- **SCOOP UP SOME ETCHED METALWARE**, such as trays, teapots, or pitchers. The patterns are subtle but glamorous and make serving a little more stylish.

Special Pattern Applications

Moroccan patterns are memorable whether carved into wood and plaster, painted on wood or pottery, etched into metal, or printed on fabrics. They are also particularly lovely when employed in zellij mosaic tile or used in elaborate embroideries. Both arts require extensive knowledge of the patterns and are extremely time-consuming. A single mosaic zellij panel may involve hundreds of tiles, while one work of embroidery of Fez may take a year or more to complete. These are crafts requiring the skill of master artisans.

Right: While zellij patterns are often seen in a multitude of bright colors, softer neutrals also have their place. They serve as a serene and yet textured backdrop for a wide variety of decorating styles. **Opposite:** *A close look at a Moroccan zellij wall provokes wonder, particularly given that each of the small shaped tiles is entirely cut by hand, requiring extreme precision. Often zellij patterns are stacked, morphing from one design to the next in a way that is surprisingly coherent and pleasing to the eye.*

ZELLIJ

Zellij (also zillij, zellije), mosaic tiling, is an art that reflects the very best in Moroccan craftsmanship and is one of the most recognizable elements in Moroccan pattern design today. In houses, zellij is most commonly seen on floors, walls, columns, fountains, and stair risers, as well as on tables, counters, and kitchen backsplashes.

Zellij is the ideal art form for Morocco for a number of reasons. In addition to the fact that Morocco is home to clay and dye materials perfect for making zellij, Morocco's Muslim religion discourages representational art but encourages geometric repetition, similar to what is found in zellij. Also, Morocco's Berber aesthetic principally involves straight lines, which reflect the principles of zellij as well. Although zellij patterns may look relatively simple, they are actually quite complex. Mathematicians are still researching the underlying mathematical rules of zellij, playing geometric catch-up with the medieval Islamic craftsmen.

Zellij dates back centuries in Morocco, and the oldest examples can be seen in the ancient Roman-influenced ruins of Volubilis, near Fez. Some say that zellij was originally brought to North Africa from Syria. The Syrians, however, did not use clay but marble tile, and this may be why the word *zellij* is used only in Morocco—its root is related to the words *zalj* (glaze) and *tazlij* (glazing). So while zellij was not invented in Morocco, Moroccan craftsmen have made it uniquely their own.

Zellij saw a boom in popularity after the fall of Islamic Spain, when Spanish refugees moved to Fez and had both the technical skills to produce zellij and the wallets to commission it. However, given zellij's complexity and expense, demand floundered over the years. Fortunately, King Hassan II was determined to preserve and put new life into Moroccan zellij making. When he came to the throne in 1961, fewer than fifty zellij craftsmen remained in the whole country. To increase their numbers, the king had a school established to teach the craft. He then set out to give these craftsmen considerable business by restoring the country's palaces that had fallen into disrepair and also ordered the use of zellij for public fountains, buildings, mosques, airports, and so forth.

Zellij in Homes

Because each tile piece is formed, baked, enameled, cut, assembled, and applied by hand, zellij is time-consuming and pricey. Historically, it was (and still is) used only by the wealthy. In Moroccan homes, zellij is usually installed on interior walls, especially the wall facing the main entrance to the house, as well as on courtyard floors, or attached to surface fountains. It may also be used on staircases and pillars and is particularly popular for tabletops. Homeowners will sometimes save up and buy a panel of zellij at a time until they have an entire staircase or wall's worth.

How Zellij Is Made

Fez is Morocco's zellij capital, and zellij artisans still use traditional methods that have been passed down from one generation to the next. Zellij requires numerous steps to go from clay to mosaic.

Forming zellij: A clay specific to Morocco is soaked for a day or so. It is then mixed by hand and cleaned before it is formed into ten-centimeter squares and dried in the sun. These squares are smoothed and trimmed into uniform bricks.

Baking zellij: The dried bricks are baked in a kiln that fires up to 1500°F (816°C).

Enameling zellij: Artisans enamel zellij. Traditional colors for zellij are yellow, blue, white, green, brown, and black. (Red is a more recent innovation, as are other colors.) Each color has a specific temperature requirement and a specific location in the kiln.

Cutting zellij: Artisans buy zellij at the market by the sack in specific colors. They then cut the colored bricks into tiles of different geometric shapes; there are more than three hundred possible shapes, and each shape has its own name. The desired shape is traced onto a brick before it is cut with a heavy chisel-edge hammer. The edges are then trimmed and polished and the back beveled to ensure that the glazed edges of each tile will fit perfectly flush. Each finished tile is called a furmeh.

Assembling zellij: Zellij panels are usually assembled in a workshop, not on-site. One panel two feet square may use hundreds of furmehs, depending on the complexity. (Some tiles are so small they must be handled with tweezers!) Most zellij makers have mastered major patterns by heart. The more complicated the pattern and the more colors, the more time-consuming it is for the zellij artisan. Individual furmehs are placed upside down and fit together like a giant puzzle. After the pattern is complete, plaster, cement, and hemp strands are used to glue the tiles together.

Applying zellij: Entire panels of zellij are moved and adhered to the wall (or other surface) with a thin layer of mortar. Difficult surfaces, like curved pillars, require tiles to be individually applied on-site.

In a zellij-making atelier in Marrakesh, the ma'allem works steadily with his apprentices. The apprentices mark each large tile with lines that will assist the ma'allem in accurately cutting them with a sharp blow of his chisel-edged hammer. The glazed blue tiles pile up to the ma'allem's side as he works.

zellij tile

- **ZELLIJ** is expensive. So it is best used where its effect may be maximized.

- **CREATE A ZELLIJ HEADBOARD**, applying it directly to the bed wall. Choose a classic shape that will never go out of style and a subtle pattern, such as all diamond shapes in two complementary colors.

- **BUY A ZELLIJ TABLE** for your terrace or porch; it will stand up to the elements. As zellij is heavy, place your table where it will seldom be moved.

- **INSTALL A ZELLIJ WALL FOUNTAIN** in your garden. These fountains are premade and can be selected to match your exterior decorating scheme.

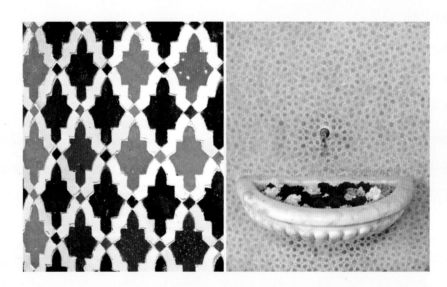

MOROCCAN EMBROIDERY

Morocco has a long and colorful history in the embroidery arts. It used to be that Moroccan girls were introduced to embroidery at a young age, studying in small groups under a ma'allema (master craftswoman). While embroiderers came from all social strata, women of the upper classes were known for embroidering their trousseaus and lovely things for their homes. Urban houses would include many embroidered pieces, particularly cushions and embroidered sheets, and owning elaborate embroideries was a status symbol.

Like other Moroccan arts, Moroccan embroideries are abstract in nature—they rarely contain figures, although small birds are sometimes seen. Most often embroidery patterns include chevrons, crosses, stars, squares, checkerboards, vines, leaves, and flowers. Floral designs are often quite abstract. Some patterns use doubled or quadrupled thread to give a more three-dimensional feel to the design. Historically, Moroccan embroidery colors are black, blue, green, red, and yellow, and the base fabrics are usually white or ivory, against which the embroidered stitches show up best.

*Left: Numbered Moroccan embroidery colors in every shade of the rainbow are pinned up in designer Ludovic Petit's Marrakesh atelier. His team of hand embroiderers are some of the city's very best. **Above:** The embroidery of Rabat is dense and massive in nature and yet curvy and feminine.*

Similar to Moroccan carpets, Moroccan embroidery patterns and styles are specific to certain cities, with distinctive designs from the cities of Fez, Rabat, Tetouan, Chefchaouen, Meknes, and Azemmour, in particular. The embroideries from the cities of Fez and Rabat are especially well known and beautiful, and have been incorporated into more contemporary interiors in recent years.

Embroideries of Fez

Perhaps the most famous of all the Moroccan embroideries, those from Fez feature intricate geometric designs in a single color. Structured and symmetrical, dense and massive, the embroideries of Fez often cover the entire fabric surface. The stitching is so careful and minute that the designs are reversible. Motifs include all manner of interlacing crosses, triangles, zigzags, chevrons, rectangles, diamonds, eight-pointed stars, flowers, vines, leaves, trees, hands, and birds. Patterns are geometric and repeat themselves and are sometimes organized into quadrants. Embroideries are usually black or deep red against a white or cream linen or cotton base.

Sadly, the number of embroiderers in Fez has decreased dramatically over the years, and the art of Fez hand embroidery is dying. Many of the most beautiful pieces of Fez embroidery are safely ensconced in museums or in the hands of private collectors who are willing to pay significant sums of money for them. It is still possible to stumble across exquisite fragments or whole pieces of Fez embroidery in the souks or in upscale antique stores, but they are quite costly.

Embroideries of Rabat

The extravagant Spanish-influenced embroideries of Morocco's capital are like flamenco dancers—seductive and enchanting. Known for their dense patterns of abstracted flowers, vines, leaves, and other plant life, Rabat embroideries are curvy and feminine, with single or multicolored patterns extending over large surfaces. Historically, blues, reds, burgundies, and yellows were commonplace in Rabat embroideries, with greens, violets, pinks, browns, and ecrus also making an occasional showing. The background of Rabat embroideries tended to be white or cream, with fine antique examples sometimes embroidered on colored net, linen, damask, or silk. Because of the dense nature of the stitch work, Rabat embroideries often appear three-dimensional, undulating across the fabric's surface

As is the case with Fez stitch work, Rabat hand embroidery is very hard to come by—an art, perhaps, relegated to Morocco's past. However, machine-embroidered versions are widely available.

Opposite: A stretch of red Moroccan embroidery in the Fez style can't fail to amaze. The embroidery covers virtually the entire surface, and a single piece can take many months to make, requiring extreme patience and an unerring attention to detail. Left: Cushions or poufs embroidered in the Rabat style in gleaming gray add a touch of unexpected sophistication to any room.

Moroccan Embroideries Today

Embroidery continues to be an important tradition in Morocco, particularly for clothing and soft home furnishings. In rural areas, Berber designs often consist of small symmetrical geometric patterns that may be found, for example, in the corners and centers of tablecloths and napkins. In urban areas, women continue to embroider edging on caftans to be worn for special occasions, while men embroider horse saddles, harnesses, poufs, double-sided bags, and babouches (slippers). Additionally, a new breed of designers—both Moroccan and Western—are using hand embroidery in new and inventive ways, including on lanterns, bedding, curtains, place mats, and more. Cotton or polyester embroidery floss is most commonly used, but more luxe designs encompass linen or silk threads, and embroidery with beads, sequins, and crystals is also sometimes featured.

Additionally, Moroccan hand-guided machine embroidery is becoming more and more prevalent. While not as fine or unique as hand embroideries, machine-made embroideries add a pretty touch to interior design and come in a wide variety of colors to suit all tastes. Machine-made versions of Fez embroideries may be found in Casablanca fabric shops sold by the yard, in dark red and black, as well as some other colors. Because of their hefty weight, they are most suitable for cushions or upholstery. Machine-made Rabat embroideries are often incorporated into premade poufs, cushions, and curtains. The most common colors are black, gold, silver, and red, almost always executed on white, ivory, or (less often) ecru.

*Top: A modern hand embroidery by a Ludovic Petit artisan incorporates beading in a luxurious touch. **Center:** Ludovic's hand-guided machine embroidery designs are dense, colorful, and playful. **Bottom:** Hand-embroidered detailing turns a Moroccan caftan into a work of art.*

moroccan embroidery

- **LAYER THE BACK OF A WINDOW SEAT** with embroidered cushions in different patterns. Consider buying different sizes as well to emphasize each cushion's unique nature.

- **PLACE TWO EMBROIDERED POUFS** in front of your fireplace for an exotic look. Since poufs are so portable, they will come in handy as extra seating.

- **PICK UP AN EMBROIDERED MARKET BASKET** online or at the souk. You can admire the handiwork while toting your groceries.

- **BUY A STACK OF INEXPENSIVE EMBROIDERED NAPKINS.** Stitch them together to make a pretty curtain or keep them stashed away in a picnic basket to add Moroccan flair to a casual lunch.

how to

STENCIL A FLOOR

Peacock Pavilions is literally filled with stenciled surfaces. It is all thanks to Melanie Royals of Royal Design Studio (see page 248), who has helped make Peacock Pavilions a more beautiful—and more patterned—place. Melanie has led several groups of talented decorative painters (now fondly known as the Peacock Painters) to decorate floors, walls, ceilings, furniture, and even our dining tent! Along the way, I have become a stencil artist myself, and I'm astonished at how easy (if time-consuming) and relatively inexpensive stenciling is!

MATERIALS

- **Tape measure**
- **Pencil**
- **Low-tack masking tape, spray adhesive, or repositionable stencil spray adhesive**
- **1 large stencil**
- **Stencil brushes**
- **Concrete paint**
- **Paper towels**
- **Sealant (polyurethane or other)**

DIRECTIONS

1. Clean the floor you'll be stenciling, and let it dry thoroughly.

2. Measure the floor to locate its center; mark it with a pencil.

3. Use masking tape or spray adhesive to position the stencil at the marked center so that it does not move while you are painting.

4. Dip a clean, dry stencil brush into the paint, and remove as much excess paint as possible from the brush by tamping it down on a stack of several paper towels.

5. Stipple (lightly tap) the stencil brush on the surface in the negative space of the stencil, working on small sections at a time. To avoid bleeding, make sure that there is only a small amount of paint on the brush at all times.

6. Use the same technique over the surface of the entire stencil.

7. Remove the stencil and reposition it. Make registration marks to line up the overall pattern adjacent to the previously stenciled area. Repeat.

8. Let the paint dry for five days, then apply a protective finish, if desired.

PART II

Living Moroccan Style

Moroccans are known for their hospitality, and entertaining dozens of people on a regular basis is common. Accordingly, Moroccan homes must work as multifunctional spaces. By day, living rooms act as gathering places for lounging on Moroccan couches, known as banquettes. For meals, tables are dressed and placed in front of the banquettes, and the space transforms into a dining room. At night, blankets are unfurled and the banquettes morph into beds. In recent years, separate living rooms, dining rooms, and bedrooms have become more commonplace. But no matter the nature or purpose of the rooms, these spaces meet the ultimate decorating challenge: striking good looks that never neglect comfort and utility. In this part, you'll decode the style secrets of some special Moroccan houses, each secret focusing on a different area of the home: living and dining rooms, bedrooms, kitchens and baths, and outdoor spaces.

MOROCCO
COURTYARDS AND GARDENS
ACHVA BENZINBERG STEIN

chapter 5

LIVING AND DINING AREAS

Most everywhere in the world, living areas are the centerpiece of the home, and the Moroccan home is no exception. Accordingly, a great deal of thought goes into making these rooms beautiful, restful, and versatile. Living areas are designed to impress and often feature the very best that the house has to offer. In newer villas, dramatic architectural features are liberally employed, making the most of lofty spaces. In older riads, craftsmanship dazzles through the use of zellij, geps, and zouak. And no matter the size of the living spaces—large or small—attention is paid to creating a feeling of abundance and warmth through layers of color and pattern and the careful use of lighting. The end result is not only comfortable but exotic.

Living Areas

In riads, living areas are marked by internal courtyards and gardens, which are either open to the sky or, if closed, at least two or three stories tall. While these central courtyard areas can serve as gracious and spacious places to spend time, they are also thoroughfares to all the connecting rooms. Therefore furnishings are placed with this in mind. Riad living and dining rooms consist of open, partially open, or closed spaces that lead off the courtyard. If the spaces are entirely exposed, they function similarly to large or small nooks around the courtyard, and although the riad may be several centuries old, the feeling is light, airy, and surprisingly modern. If the rooms are partially exposed, they are cozier in feel, with archways that open to the courtyard. If the rooms are closed, they are typically long and narrow, punctuated by a tall door in the middle that leads into and out of the courtyard. A room off the courtyard can become multidimensional with curtains hung in archways, allowing for an open and bright feel or a snug and cozy ambiance, depending on the season and the mood.

Mimicking the grandeur of internal riad courtyards, villas often have central great rooms with unusually high ceilings (twelve feet or higher), or domes. Often, open arched doorways link several rooms together in the villa, including one or more living rooms, dens, and dining rooms. The space typically connects to the front door by a foyer. Smaller villas are bungalow-style with more conventional and modest-sized living spaces. That is also the case for living areas in Moroccan apartments, with the exception of those in buildings from the colonial era, which may have larger living rooms with lovely, fine fittings.

Previous pages, left: The voluminous main space in Stephanie's villa includes an arched arcade around a central courtyard, mimicking those found in riads. The roof can be canopied or opened up to the sky. A huge wax bowl with floating flowers substitutes for a fountain, and leather poufs make for comfortable seating. Previous pages, right: The great room of our Medina Pavilion features a cluster of antique lanterns. A hand-carved, eight-sided table purchased in the Marrakesh souks has pride of place. Turquoise pottery from Tamegroute can be found clustered around the room. Opposite: In a guest salon at Peacock Pavilions, a key-holed doorway provides an oversized entry. The couch is draped casually with a Moroccan-striped fouta and filled with cushions made from vintage textiles. Large poufs serve as additional seating around the coffee table made from an old Moroccan window (see How to Make a Coffee Table from a Moroccan Window, page 128). Left: The living room in John's Essaouira apartment is a generous space anchored by a fireplace at one end. Over the glazed bejmat tiled floor is a woolly Berber carpet, which John found in Mustapha's Carpet Emporium in Essaouira. The central seating space is made up of a banquette-like couch and two kilim-covered armchairs. A trio of modern tables provides plenty of space for objects.

*Above: A Moroccan banquette is loaded with vintage cushions in the Marrakesh home of photographer Delphine Warin. The carpet is hand-embroidered raffia, a specialty of artisans in northern Morocco. **Right:** A seating area with a Moroccan banquette looks super fresh in Kamal's riad. The tiled lower walls and floors make for a lively backdrop. **Following page:** The living room in Anne's Marrakesh riad is kitted out in sophisticated bohemian style. A charcoal and lavender palette and plenty of banquette seating invite guests to stay a while.*

THE MOROCCAN SALON AND THE MOROCCAN BANQUETTE

The heart of the traditional Moroccan living space is known as the Moroccan salon, the name undoubtedly harkening back to the French protectorate. The Moroccan salon is easily recognized because it features a particular form of seating called the Moroccan banquette—a low-slung backless couch used side by side in multiples and made to hug the walls. Depending on the room and the position of windows, doors, and fireplaces, banquettes typically run along three walls, forming a U shape, or along two walls, forming an L shape. Banquettes are custom-built pieces made to fit a room's particular dimensions, maximizing space and providing comfortable seating for many people. This form of living room is particularly useful in traditional Moroccan riads, where rooms are generally long and narrow, making relatively few seating arrangements possible. It is not uncommon to have more than one space in a riad with banquette seating, given its practicality.

As for the banquettes themselves, they are usually made up of several parts: a wooden base that is either plain or carved, with arch-shaped cutouts or inlay detailing painted with intricate patterns; an upholstered long, narrow mattress that is placed on top of the base and serves as the seat; and a back that is not fixed but made up of multiple cushions that rest directly against the wall. Given their size and the number of cushions, traditional banquettes are formal affairs. These days, many craftsmen are making smaller banquettes for cozier spots. Rather than seating for fifteen or more, a smaller banquette can provide seating for just three or four, similar to a couch but always abutting a wall.

FURNISHINGS AND SEATING ARRANGEMENTS

Because of the shape of Moroccan salons and the ample seating of the banquettes, multiple small tea tables are often more practical than one large coffee table. Tea tables are portable (requiring only one person to move them) and thus can be easily reconfigured as needed. These tables are frequently round, eight-sided, or even star-shaped. They can be carved, have cutouts on the sides, or be painted with intricate designs. They are most often wood, but can also be made of brass. Sometimes they are simply trays placed on collapsing wood or metal stands.

While villas generally have living rooms that are wider than those found in riads and dars (therefore making several seating arrangements possible), many will still have a Moroccan salon. Additionally, a "European salon" with freestanding couches is common. Quite a few European salons feature seating that adapts the banquette by adding a fixed back, thereby blending both Western and Moroccan traditions. Other key seating includes poufs. These traditional round or square leather ottomans are found in most Moroccan homes. Poufs are embroidered or plain, and more recent versions are made of fabric, rather than leather. They mix well with contemporary and traditional furniture alike and can also double as small tables.

Beyond Moroccan and European salons, just as in the West, many homes in Morocco have other areas where plenty of living is done. These more intimate spaces have specific purposes, such as a room for TV viewing or reading or a playroom for children. These each have their own seating needs, depending on use, frequently with less formal arrangements but no fewer Moroccan influences.

moroccan-inspired seating areas

- **CREATE A MOROCCAN BANQUETTE** in your own living room by placing a twin mattress on wooden pallets. Layer on sabra fabrics and embroidered cushions for a snug and inviting feel.

- **PLACE A PAIR OF MATCHING POUFS** in front of the fireplace. Not only are they the ideal perch for roasting marshmallows, but they can be easily moved when extra seating is needed.

- **FORGO A LARGER COFFEE TABLE** and use two or three tea tables instead. They're convenient because they can be used in multiple configurations.

- **CREATE A GYPSY ATMOSPHERE** by placing a dressed mattress directly on the floor for seating. With a plush carpet underneath you and cushions behind you, floor seating becomes comfortable for evening lounging.

ACCESSORIZING LIVING AREAS

Just as the perfect handbag completes an outfit, so, too, do accessories complete a room! Moroccan homes incorporate strategically placed small furnishings and objects to provide panache on even the smallest budget.

Pottery vases, bowls, and platters, whether plain, tadelakt, or patterned, are used to hold fresh flowers, to corral small objects, to cluster on shelves, and so much more. Meanwhile, etched metalware, including trays, boxes, and pails, works hard in living spaces, performing all sorts of sundry tasks while reflecting light and adding another dimension to the room.

Soft furnishings, including cushions and textiles, are liberally used in Moroccan homes and transform the feeling of banquettes and couches in an instant. There is an ever-changing variety of cushions, including those that are flat weaves, embroidered, and sequined. They look particularly good when amassed for effect. Morocco's many textiles sold throughout souks in the country are also very useful in this regard. These are used as blankets, hangings, and loose upholstery, and provide a great deal of color, pattern, and texture. They also make up the cultural heritage of the country, passing on various tribal traditions.

Rugs, whether pile or flat weave, and rug making are also a vital part of Morocco's history and tradition. Each rug has a story to tell, and many are filled with talismanic symbols. Beyond their rich meanings, rugs are like artwork for the floor, setting the tone for the entire room. Indeed, in either rich hues or creamy shades, rugs are perhaps the quickest of the quick-change artists in the Moroccan design spectrum. Often, multiple rugs can be found in the same room. Flat-weave rugs may overlap, so it is unclear where one carpet ends and another begins.

Lighting—bejeweled, pierced, or with colored panes—also has an uncanny ability to turn any room

into a more intriguing space. Hung singly or in multiples, lanterns add real star power to a room. The larger the room and the higher the ceiling, the greater the possibilities that lighting can be clustered for impact. Flat-bottomed lanterns set on the floor or placed on a table, or carried with candles inside, are also very popular and romantic. These act as great hurricane lights as well.

Opposite: A fantastic collection of vintage Moroccan memorabilia adds a splash of color to Yann's walls. The embroidered cushions with their geometric patterns provide some modern sensibility to the mix. *Left:* A pink, red, and white vintage Moroccan rug provides instant cheer in my children's playroom at Peacock Pavilions. I've accessorized it with Moroccan blankets and cushions, a tea table, and poufs. *Below, left:* A jumble of Moroccan cushions made from vintage blankets looks cozy on this daybed. *Below right:* A vintage handira draped over a banquette is all it takes to create instant texture.

moroccan accessories in the living area

- **ROLL OUT A MOROCCAN BLANKET** on your floor, instead of a rug. They're heavy and will lie flat, and the price is right!

- **CHOOSE AN AREA** of your living room that has open wall space to feature a pierced metal lantern. The empty space will highlight to full advantage the intricate lacy shadows the lantern throws off.

- **HANG A LARGE MOROCCAN LANTERN** over a seating area. Lanterns mix surprisingly well with any decor and help center the room.

- **COLLECT METALWARE** in different shapes and sizes. Group them on a console, or on a side table on a tray, or layer them on a fireplace mantel.

WEST HEIDELBERG
DOUGHARTY RD
BULLEEN VIA NTH
LA TROBE UNIVERSITY
GARDEN CITY VIA PORT MELB
PORT MELB
NTH KEW BURKE
KEW EARL
KEW
NORTH KEW BELFORD ROAD
CITY
FLINDERS ST
NICHOLSON &
QUEENS BRIDGE VIA INGLES ST
QUEENS BRIDGE VIA LORIMER ST
QUEENS BRIDGE
FISHERMAN'S
VIA INGLES ST
FISHERMAN'S
VIA LORIMER ST
FISHERMENS
PRINCES BRIDGE
LORIMER ST
CANAL
ST

A Berber carpet provides graphic grounding in my living room.

how to

MAKE A COFFEE TABLE FROM A MOROCCAN WINDOW

Window frames can be easily converted into tables, and those with decorative metal grilles are particularly appropriate. Most Moroccan window frames have been repainted several times throughout the years, and the underlying colors show through from chips and scratches, adding a nice texture to the piece. Moroccan windows come in many sizes, but they are rarely large enough to make into a dining table; dining tables are best made from an old door. (The steps are similar to those for creating a window coffee table.)

MATERIALS

- Vintage window frame
- Sandpaper
- Paint, stain, or varnish (optional)
- Wood for legs
- Circular saw
- Corner bracket angles to attach legs
- Electric drill
- Wood screws
- Screwdriver
- Table leg levelers/feet (optional)
- Glass tabletop, cut to size (optional)
- ½-inch x ¾-inch wood strips (optional)

PREPARATION

If necessary, sand the window frame and either stain or paint it. You can choose to simply leave it as is, too. Clean the surface before moving on.

DIRECTIONS

1. Consider the dimensions of the window frame when sizing the legs. They should not be too spindly or too beefy—proportion is the key. Most legs are well proportioned at 3 inches (7.5 cm) square, but use your judgment and taste. The wood you use should be similar to the wood in the frame, unless the window is painted, in which case you may choose to paint the legs to match. The height of the table must be considered; 18 to 22 inches (46 to 56 cm) is fairly standard, but measure other tables to get the exact height you desire. Remember to consider the table leg levelers (see step 3) when cutting the length of wood for the legs with a circular saw. Sand and bevel the bottom of the wood legs slightly to give them a more finished appearance.

2. Fasten the legs to the window frame with the metal brackets. Follow the instructions on the package for installation. It is best to drill pilot holes in the wood so the screws do not split it. The pilot hole should be ⅟₃₂ to ⅟₁₆ inch (1 to 2 mm) smaller than the screw diameter and is necessary if using a hard wood versus a soft wood, such as pine.

3. If using, fasten the leg levelers/feet. Adjustable leg levelers/feet may be purchased at most hardware stores and help to balance the table on uneven surfaces (or if you accidentally make one of the legs slightly shorter than the others). Attach per instructions on the package.

4. If you want an inset glass tabletop, it will need to sit on a lip or edge support. Cut thin strips of wood approximately ¾ inch (1.9 cm) tall and ½ inch (1.3 cm) wide. Fasten them with screws below the top edge of the window frame, so that they can support the glass. These strips of wood can be painted or varnished to complement the window frame.

5. Place the glass on top of the table. Give it a final wipe-down and place the table in the location of your choice.

NOTE: The tabletop glass should be ¼ inch to 5/16 inches (6 to 8 mm) thick, depending on the size of the window frame. (Consult with a glass supplier for a recommendation on thickness.) Measure the size carefully, as glass cannot be shaved like wood, and vintage window frames are often slightly out of square. You might consider making a template out of cardboard or kraft paper to bring to the glass supplier. Have the glass edges polished and, for a sophisticated touch, beveled.

Dining Areas

Although meals and mealtimes are extremely important to Moroccans (no standing in the kitchen having a
sandwich on the go here!), dining areas are not always
at the top of the list in home planning. Nonetheless,
dining Moroccan–style has its appeal, and lessons can
be gleaned that you can take home with you.

FURNISHINGS AND SEATING ARRANGEMENTS

Unlike in Europe or North America, dedicated dining
rooms are not a standard part of traditional Moroccan
homes, particularly in riads and dars. More typically, a
large tea table in the living room will serve double duty
as a dining table. Poufs or stools will be added around
the table to complete the seating when it's mealtime.
Alternatively, a light, round table will be moved to the
L-shaped corner of two abutting banquettes, and when
the meal is over, the table will be folded up and stored.
While this sort of makeshift dining room is flexible and
breeds conviviality, it is not always convenient, as storage is necessary and people can get a bit cramped.

Morocco residents also get creative in other ways,
sometimes using the wide hallways in riads and dars
as dining rooms or temporarily repurposing library
or foyer tables. These are all good options for dining, particularly for apartment dwellers, given the
limited space and the necessity of multifunctionality.
For those riads and dars that have a larger courtyard
area or central space, one corner is often dedicated to
dining. This gives a contemporary, loftlike feel, as the
space above is open. An added bonus is that when the
weather is good, diners can see the stars overhead. On
a more practical level, seating at a proper dining table
is generally more comfortable than banquette seating.
The dining area is typically placed close to the kitchen
to allow for easy serving and clearing.

Many modernized riads and dars also have converted rooms to serve as permanent dining rooms on
the first floor of the home. Similar to those in the West,
these dining rooms are generally entered through one
or more open doorways, but in keeping with Moroccan
architectural style, the doorways are frequently arched.
Large dining tables are made or bought to accommodate the characteristically long, narrow rooms found
in these old medina houses. With a greater European
influence, villas often have wider and airier dining
rooms, almost always abutting the kitchen. Whether in
a riad, an apartment, or a villa, dining tables are typically made of wood, zellij tile, or contemporary molded
plastic. Seating runs the gamut of chair options, from
very traditional to very modern. On the floor, patterned
tile often substitutes for carpets.

Previous pages, left: A Moroccan coffee table doubles as a dining table in the Marrakesh home of designers Julie and Moulay. A pouf and banquette provide requisite seating. Previous pages, right: John's dining table is located in a wide hallway in his apartment. By day it displays books, which John's dog, Mr. Pico, carefully guards. On the floor is a vintage carpet and overhead a series of lanterns John designed. A wooden armoire with mashrabiya and mirrored arches stores table linens. Below, left: Sylvain uses modern lighting and seating as well as fun cement tile to add a youthful feel to his historic Essaouira riad. Right: Anne's modern dining room is a corner of the courtyard in her Marrakesh riad.

moroccan-inspired dining areas

- **TURN A CARVED DOOR INTO A DINING TABLE.** Attach four legs and place a piece of glass on top to protect the wood carvings and create a perfectly flat surface.

- **CONVERT YOUR COFFEE TABLE** into a dining table and use poufs for seating. This Moroccan touch is a particularly good solution for space-constrained apartments.

- **INVEST IN A ZELLIJ TILE TABLE** for the dining room. Make sure that it won't have to be moved often, as these tables are very heavy.

- **CONSTRUCT AN ARCHED OPEN DOORWAY** to your dining room. This simple architectural feature creates a Moroccan mood on entering and exiting the room, no matter the furnishings.

ACCESSORIZING DINING AREAS

Dining is a favorite pastime of most Moroccans, and there is often a crowd invited to enjoy couscous on Fridays, the equivalent of Sundays for many. Along with friends and family, there are a number of accessories that make a regular showing in Moroccan dining rooms. On the table itself, pottery and porcelain are standard. The tagine with its conical lid is the iconic dish of the country. Single portion–sized tagines are a relatively new contribution to the market and give place settings a structured look. A distinct brilliant shade, such as red, makes a statement in tableware. Hand-painted patterns are also plentiful in table linens.

Hanging over the dining table is Moroccan lighting. If ever there was a space suitable for this sort of illumination, the dining room is it! As Moroccan lanterns are principally designed for ambiance, they are perfect for sultry evening lighting, and all the better for dining. Depending on the size and shape of the dining table, one or several lanterns will cascade down from the ceiling in a Moroccan home. Pierced lighting is especially lovely as it casts exquisite tattoolike patterns down below. There is also a wide range of sconces and lamps for lighting the sideboard.

Under the dining room table, a cozy carpet is always appropriate. Moroccans are spoiled with choices ranging from stark minimalist designs to complex patterns. Flat weaves are easy to maintain, and most Moroccans just give them a vigorous shake outdoors for cleaning after mealtime. Pile carpets feel wonderful underfoot and provide a luxuriousness that is hard to beat. The color palette leaves little to be desired, from creamy beiges to rich reds and so much more. Sizing can be tricky, though, as many carpets are designed for long, narrow rooms and can't always be found in standard sizes.

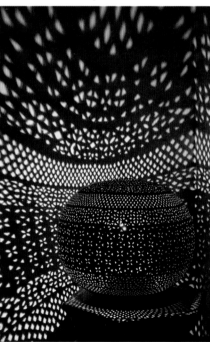

Opposite, left: A table is set with Moroccan red-patterned porcelain of Marrakesh shop owner Corinne Bensimon's own design. **Opposite, center:** A pierced lantern at Marrakesh restaurant Tanjia casts intriguing patterns across walls and floors. **Opposite, right:** A vintage Moroccan rug is the star attraction in Corinne's Marrakesh villa. **Left:** The table in my dining room at Peacock Pavilions was designed by my architect husband and custom made by a woodworker in Morocco's capital city of Rabat. The chairs and benches are upholstered with old Moroccan carpet fragments. Hanging over the table is a series of small lanterns that I designed for my shop, Red Thread Souk.

moroccan accessories in the dining area

- **HANG ONE OR MORE PIERCED LANTERNS** over your dining room table. The filtered light will obviate the need for candles and create a mysterious ambiance.

- **DRESS YOUR DINING ROOM TABLE** with platters and plates in blue and white. To create interest, use different patterns, such as those found on pottery from the cities of Fez and Safi.

- **UPHOLSTER YOUR DINING ROOM CHAIRS** with carpet fragments or blankets. Use patterns in saffrons and reds, which will hide spills.

- **SPLURGE ON A FANTASTICALLY PATTERNED RUG** for your dining room. It will be sure to get noticed by guests and set the stage for your dining table.

how to

MAKE AN ALL-NATURAL, MOROCCAN-INSPIRED FURNITURE POLISH

As Peacock Pavilions is located in a working olive grove with trees that are a century old, I have found many good ways to use our olive oil. It is amazing how easy it is to make your own cleaning products with a few ingredients from your kitchen. Use this furniture polish only on unpainted wood.

INGREDIENTS

- 3 cups (750 ml) olive oil
- 1 cup (250 ml) white vinegar

DIRECTIONS

1. Pour the oil and vinegar into a jar with a lid.

2. Close the lid tightly and shake well.

3. Apply a small amount of the oil mixture to a soft rag and buff the furniture.

4. Let the surface dry for an hour or so before using, so that all the goodness can seep in.

NOTE: Store the polish at room temperature in a dark place. Make a fresh batch each month. This polish can also be made using 2 cups (500 ml) of olive oil and the juice from one large lemon.

chapter 6

BEDROOMS

Bedrooms are undoubtedly the dreamiest place in any home and particularly good spots to add an infusion of Moroccan style. For those who prefer bedrooms that act as serene and calming retreats, there is a great range of textiles and carpets available in soft whites and ivories, and creamy beiges and taupes. For those who prefer bedrooms of the dramatic and mysterious type, patterned plush rugs, bohemian daybeds, and saturated wall treatments are in order. No matter the style, delicate and moody illumination from pierced lanterns seems tailor-made for overhead bedroom lighting.

138

Architectural Styles and Finishes

Traditionally, Moroccan bedrooms were simply the living rooms, which transformed themselves at night. However, increasingly there are dedicated rooms for that imperative evening pastime: sleeping. Because of the architectural makeup of riads and dars, bedrooms are almost always of the long and narrow variety. This means that the bed is usually placed in one of the two narrow ends of the room facing inward, bisecting the space. There are only slender openings on either side, and a long open area at the foot of the bed. The limited floor plans in medina houses present a few decorating challenges.

In addition to the rooms' being narrow, the ceilings are generally quite lofty. As ceilings are not forgotten in the Moroccan decorative tradition, homeowners highlight this space in special ways. Crown molding made out of sculpted geps makes a showing, and the carved plasterwork can even extend over the entire ceiling in the most elaborate rooms. Exposed structural beams add character, and reeds nested above the rafters layer on more interest. Ceilings are coffered, vaulted, peaked, or domed. Painted designs twist and swirl across wide swaths, taking eyes on a mystery tour. These special ceiling treatments are particularly lovely to admire when lying in bed.

In terms of flooring, unglazed or glazed bejmat tile gives a bedroom an elegant look. These tiles can be laid simply or in a herringbone pattern for a bit more polish. Bejmat borders and plinths running around the edging finish the floor off neatly. Dess is also used, sometimes with patterns made with inlaid bejmat tile. Patterned cement tiling is particularly common on floors, adding life and charm to the whole

room. Graphic black and white tiles add punch, while colored patterned tiles convey a more free-spirited attitude.

As for walls, they, too, get individual attention. Unlike in the West, wallpaper is rare (and always imported), perhaps because handmade finishes are feasible and craftsmen are abundant. Tadelakt treatments in the bedroom are especially coveted. They glow and appear to emit beautiful light in warm white or pale gray. Bedrooms seem to lend themselves in particular to modern Moroccan bohemian style. Walls are often painted a rich shade, such as turquoise, cobalt, saffron, or red. The color may even extend to the ceiling, sure to help enhance even the most multihued dreams. Alternatively, white may form the neutral base for creating charming gallery walls, with a multitude of personal paintings, drawings, and treasures thrifted in the souks displayed.

Contributing a distinct Moroccan appeal to bedrooms are the windows and doors. These are typically not of the run-of-the-mill variety but rather are unique architectural features in and of themselves. Doors and windows, even in the bedroom, tend to be oversized, leaving a lasting impression. Because of their size, double doors are typical, and if arched are reminiscent of butterflies when open. Further enhancing their decorative appeal, they can incorporate Moorish shapes or painted patterns. Bedroom doors and windows often include latticework or multiple panes to soften direct views for privacy reasons; these have the added advantage of casting beautiful, complex shadows onto floors, walls, and ceilings.

Previous pages, left: Patterned cement tiles add tremendous character to Stefan's master bedroom in his Essaouira riad. A vintage striped Moroccan blanket on the bed is paired with a leopard-patterned headboard. Two small tea tables flank the bed in the narrow room.
Previous pages, right: I tweaked the idea of Moroccan embellished ceilings in this guest room at Peacock Pavilions. The design was commissioned from Modello Designs and based on a fragment of antique embroidery. The carpet is vintage Moroccan and the bedspread is a hand-embroidered piece I purchased in Rajasthan. Opposite, left: French stylist Aurelia put down a cement-tiled floor in her baby girl's bedroom in Marrakesh. The pattern adds another fun element to this colorful room. Opposite, center: Stripes on a bedspread and a boldly patterned cement tile marry well in a guest bedroom in Sylvain's riad. Opposite, right: The walls in Rose's bedroom are finished in a feminine lilac tadelakt. On the bed and floor are vintage Moroccan rag rugs. The silver pouf is by French designer Ludovic Petit. Left: The focus is on textures in this guest room at Peacock Pavilions. On the bed is a vintage handira. The lanterns are my own design, incorporating handwoven fabrics, and the cushions are machine embroidered in the Rabat style. On the wall is a series of Arabic calligraphy plaques made by my father. I commissioned the stenciled ceiling design from Royal Design Studio; it is modeled after a bone-inlaid dresser I fell in love with.

moroccan-inspired bedrooms

- **EXPERIMENT WITH COLOR** on your bedroom walls. Consider using a glaze or a gloss over the paint to deepen the effect.

- **PAINT OR STENCIL** your bedroom door with a pattern. If this is too complicated, consider wallpapering one or both sides.

- **CUT WOODEN LATTICE STRIPS** and apply in a wide crisscross pattern over your window. Depending on the sun and your proximity to neighbors, you may be able to dispense with shades or curtains.

- **LAY BEJMAT** or other rectangular tile on your floor in a neutral color. It will serve as a refined backdrop for your carpets.

MOROCCAN MAGIC
AND WEAVING

Weaving has mystical implications in Moroccan culture. The act of weaving is thought to have baraka (divine qualities), and wool is believed to be naturally baraka-filled. The loom with warp strings is also believed to have a spirit and to possess magical traits, and the powers of the loom begin before it is even built! Some Berbers are said to believe that those who step over warp threads before they are attached to the loom risk lives filled with bad luck. Once the loom is built, superstitious Berber weavers use salt—which is believed to be powerful in warding off genies—to dust the loom and the area around it. In some Berber tribes, a girl entering puberty steps under and through a loom to tie up her virginity. Before she is married, she must repeat the process to be "untied." Tying a warp thread around the head of a sick person is also said to speed his or her recovery.

BEDS

The heart of every bedroom is, of course, the bed! Moroccan beds frequently look like oversized banquettes, with mattresses placed directly on low wooden bases. These bases can be very simple, if they are covered by blankets, or they can be quite ornate if they are made to be seen. Ornate options include mashrabiyas, inlaid mosaic work, hand carvings, and arched cutouts. Alternatively, it is not unusual for mattresses to be placed directly on a raised fixed cement slab, sometimes with a tadelakt surface. These are normally constructed when the rooms are being built and blend right into the cement floor. In a yet more bohemian style, mattresses might be placed directly on the floor. More alluring Moroccan-inspired beds feature headboards made out of mosaic zellij or sculpted geps plasterwork, installed right on the wall. They can also be inset in an alcove with a vaulted ceiling, adding further drama.

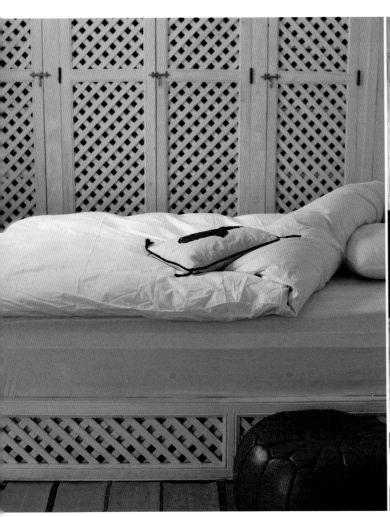

For bedding, there are numerous options. Handiras (wedding blankets) with sequins catch the light and pair perfectly with white or ivory sheets. They are glamorous and organic at the same time—an unbeatable combination. Meanwhile, colorful sabra bedspreads give a bed a gypsy caravan–like feel. Sabra is typically striped but can also be found in larger blocks of color. For those who prefer something a bit more neutral or masculine, there are plenty of handwoven woolen blankets on offer. These blankets usually come in ivory, taupe, and soft black and often have pom-poms along the borders to add detail and character. Additionally, smaller carpets easily substitute as unique throws at the foot of the bed. These are available in a panoply of patterns and shades, and you are sure to find one to go with your decor. In terms of throw pillows, layer a pile of vintage flat-weave cushions for a look that's one-of-a-kind ethnic. Delicate hand- or machine-embroidered cushions are also sure to do the trick and come in a stunning array of designs.

Opposite, left: In a bedroom at Dar Rumi, the bed is an oversized Moroccan banquette made with lattice wood strips. The lattice is picked up again for the built-in wall of closets. The red leather pouf provides a shot of contrasting color. **Opposite, right:** *A twin mattress is simply placed on the floor and covered with vibrant handwoven sabra cloth in French interior designer Ludovic Petit's bedroom.* **Left:** *A wedding blanket on a bed goes perfectly with a creamy vintage Moroccan carpet on the floor, creating a serene bedroom atmosphere.*

It's all about earth tones in this tiny guest bedroom at the Marrakesh villa of stylist and shop owner Corinne Bensimon. A handwoven Berber all-wool chocolate blanket with pompoms is paired with a deep burgundy throw with a whipstitch detail. The hand-painted linen cushions are sold in Corinne's Marrakesh shop, Lilah Spirit, as is the oversized artwork. A small Beni Ourain carpet with a modern zigzag looks as if it were custom-made for the room.

BRINGING IT HOME

the moroccan bed

- **HANG A CARPET** to serve as a bed's headboard to create instant drama. Alternatively, use one as a canopy for your bed and decipher the talismanic symbols while gazing straight up.

- **DRAPE A SEQUINED HANDIRA** (wedding blanket) at the foot of the bed. The three-dimensional nature of these textiles adds texture without color for those who prefer a more serene-looking bedroom.

- **IN CHILDREN'S ROOMS**, use fun, striped sabra cloths as bedspreads. These can be thrown in the washing machine for easy cleaning.

- **INVEST IN A SMALL FLAT-WEAVE CARPET.** It can do double duty as a bed throw or a bedside carpet, depending on your mood.

Furniture, Surfaces, and Accessories

Other than the bed, Moroccan bedrooms often have relatively little furniture because much of it is built directly into the room. Closets, shelves, and drawers are normally on one side of the bedroom, discreetly hidden behind doors. Shelving will sometimes be exposed so as to allow for easy access to certain objects. Because of the narrow nature of bedrooms in riads and dars, bedside tables are small and narrow. Tea tables are a good choice to double as nightstands, given their size. Some tables have hollowed-out tops, helpful to ensure that objects don't fall off in such tight quarters. Tables with lacy brass or intricate inlaid bone detailing add a sublime touch to the room.

On bedroom floors (and anywhere in the Moroccan home), wall-to-wall carpeting is unheard-of. However, the vast spectrum ensures that every bedroom has one that's just right. The hand-knotted ivory carpets from the Atlas Mountains, highly textured and plush, lend themselves well to sultry bedroom decor. Dramatic black-and-white lattice Tazenakht carpets give a Morocco-meets-Hollywood feel. For the more adventurous, patterned carpets with mysterious talismanic symbols, in shades of pink, red, or gold, are made to enchant. Curtains may feature hand- or machine-embroidery in Moroccan patterns. Or long lengths of sabra can serve this purpose, the threads gleaming as they block out the sun's rays. Overhead, large lanterns in shimmery brass or a never-tarnishing maillechort cast enticing patterns all around the room. For a more bohemian look, multiple lanterns can hang in varying lengths from the ceiling, some with colored glass panes. Alternatively, delicate Moroccan sconces are best used in tight-fitting spaces.

Opposite, above: *The exposed closet and shelving unit in Dar Rumi's master bedroom acts as a focal point of the room. The simple Moorish-inspired shapes are pleasing to the eye and show off the owner's jewel-colored caftan collection. White containers and baskets from Zara Home are used to store accessories.* Opposite, below: *A quilt is draped over a wool Moroccan blanket with pom-poms in Geraldine and David's Marrakesh villa. Striped vintage blankets are also laid on the floors— an inexpensive carpet alternative. A hollowed-out Moroccan tea table corrals the morning coffee.* Left: *A four-poster bed draped with a green sari is the star attraction in John's master bedroom. But playing an important secondary role is his fantastic collection of vintage Moroccan carpets, each with intriguing symbols, colors, and patterns. Two serve as artwork for the floor, while a third works as a throw at the end of the bed, layered over a sequined bedspread. The walls are in beige tadelakt.*

Mixing It Up

Stylish Moroccan homeowners are influenced by their travels, trends, and decorating magazines. So except in hotels or guest riads, it is rare to see a complete Moroccan look in the bedroom. Indeed, bedrooms with a fusion of Moroccan and other influences are perhaps the most interesting—a reflection of the journeys and the likes of those who sleep in them. Crystal chandeliers might mix with handiras, and American pop art might balance out bejmat floors. Tadelakt walls might blend with gilt headboards, while mirrored nightstands might flank banquette beds. And just as midcentury modern furniture seems a perfect match for carpets from the Atlas Mountains, so, too, do Swedish armoires harmonize flawlessly with Moroccan embroidered cushions. The combinations are limited only by the imagination.

Below, left: In Helmut's Marrakesh riad, a fantastically colored and textured vintage Moroccan rug manages to be the perfect floor covering for a bedroom filled with Italian and Chinese antiques as well as contemporary furnishings and artwork. Below, right: In Sylvain's guest bedroom in his Essaouira riad, his love of pop art marries seamlessly with a graphic tile floor, a brightly colored sabra bedspread, and two yellow tadelakt-finished lamps.

moroccan accessories in the bedroom

- **PUT A PILE CARPET** on your bedroom floor. This is particularly important in children's rooms, as kids like to hang out on the floor.

- **MAKE DOUBLE CURTAINS OUT OF HAIKS**—long lengths of ivory or white handwoven fabric. Simply fling one side over the rod and admire the filtered light it creates.

- **CREATE STORAGE** by hanging colorful market baskets on a series of pegs in children's bedrooms. Kids can stash art supplies, sports equipment, and sundry items inside, making cleanup fun and easy.

- **CONSIDER USING PIERCED LANTERNS** as overhead lighting in the bedroom. It's atmospheric and makes for the ultimate in romantic lighting.

 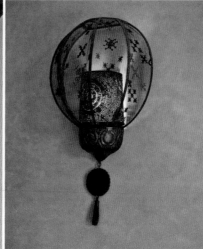

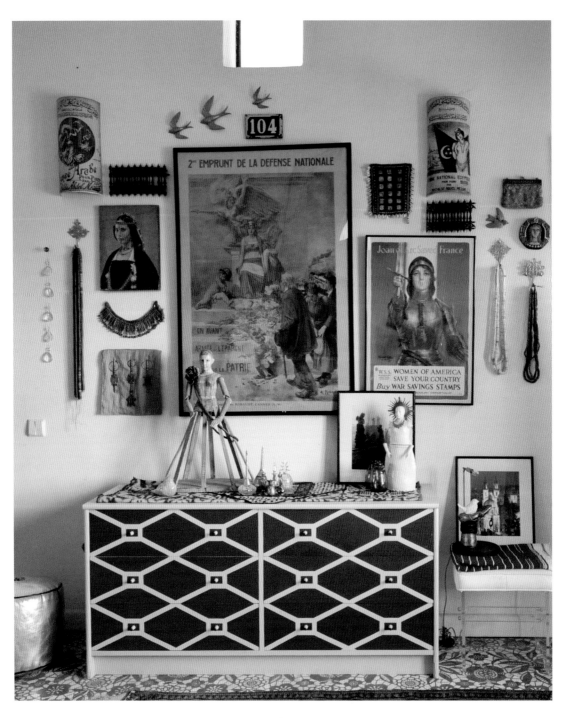

Thrifted treasures from the souks adorn
my bedroom walls.

These hand-embroidered pillows are
designed by Ludovic Petit. So pretty.

how to

MAKE A HEADBOARD USING A WEDDING BLANKET

As a longtime admirer of sequined handiras—those confections made by Berber tribes to protect brides—I am always looking for new ways to use and display them. Turning one into a headboard is a glamorous solution!

MATERIALS

- ¼-inch (6.35 mm) plywood cut to fit the size of your bed. (While any shape is feasible, a basic rectangle is recommended, as this will be the shape of the handira, and the focus of the headboard will most likely be on the blanket's sparkle and texture.)
- 2-inch (5-cm)-thick foam, cut to the size of the headboard
- Marker
- Utility knife
- Scissors
- Batting sized to the headboard, plus 6 inches (15 cm) on each side (to wrap around the foam and plywood)
- Handira (wedding blanket)
- Staple gun and staples
- Flush mounts
- Drill

PREPARATION

Size the plywood to fit the bed. The headboard should be slightly wider than your mattress. Remember that the padding and foam will add to the width (usually less than 1 inch [2.5 cm]). The height of the headboard is up to you, but consider the size of your handira.

DIRECTIONS

1. Lay the foam on the ground and place the cut plywood headboard on top. Then trace the shape onto the foam using a marker. Cut the shape out using a utility knife.

2. Cut the batting, leaving at least 6 inches (15 cm) on all sides to wrap around the foam and plywood.

3. Cut the handira as needed; it should be the same size as the batting. It should be large enough to cover the foam, plywood, and batting, and the blanket should be able to wrap around the front of the headboard to the back.

4. To put the headboard together, you will need a large, clean, flat work surface (a clean floor works fine). Place the handira on your work surface right side down.

5. Place the batting on top of the handira. Lay the foam on top of the batting, then place the plywood on top. You should have all four layers sandwiched together. Be sure to line up the foam and plywood and have enough blanket fabric and batting around the edges to be able to pull

the two up and around to the back of the plywood. Begin attaching the fabric and batting over the back of the plywood by using a staple gun. Staple it with ¼-inch (6-mm) staples placed every 2 inches (5 cm). Put two staples into the center of two opposite sides and then repeat on the top and bottom. Now flip the entire headboard around to see if the fabric is sitting right. If so, flip it back over and staple out from the center, alternating from side to side and top to bottom. If the handira is not positioned correctly, pull the staples out, adjust it, and start over.

6. Trim any excess material and batting with scissors.

7. To hang the headboard, keep in mind the height of your bed before you attach flush mounts to the back of your headboard and to the wall. You will slide the halves together to create an interlocking and stable mount. To install them, first locate the studs on your wall behind where the headboard will be placed. Attach the bottom part of the flush mounts to the wall and into the studs as far apart as possible within the width of the headboard. Hold the headboard against the wall to mark the location of the receiving mount on it. Take the headboard away, drill the holes for the mounts, and attach the mounts facing down. Lift the headboard onto the wall mounts to secure it. Finally, move your mattress and bed frame back against the wall and your new headboard.

chapter 7

KITCHENS, BATHS, AND TRANSITIONAL SPACES

Kitchens, baths, and transitional areas (entries, hallways, and staircases) are perhaps the most utilitarian parts of any Moroccan home, but that doesn't mean they are lacking in charm. Indeed, a little Moroccan flair goes a long way in making these spaces more appealing, and in ways that do not depend on expensive appliances and fittings. The key is focusing on handmade and touchable materials and paying particular attention to color and pattern.

158

Kitchens

Kitchens in Moroccan homes tend to be smaller than their North American counterparts. In most riads, kitchen size is significantly constrained by courtyard size, as the two share adjoining spaces and the courtyard always trumps in importance. This means that riad kitchens are reduced to tucked-away corners of the house. Accordingly, there is very little counter and cabinet space, and storage is quite limited. Sinks and appliances are often not full-sized, and some homes even forgo ovens. These spaces are typically quite dark, as light is just provided through the entryway or, if the homeowner is lucky, an additional interior window.

Because of their diminutive size, most Moroccan kitchens have open shelving. Given that kitchenware is necessarily visible, many homeowners use this as an opportunity to display their dishes artfully. This also functions as an incentive to pare down and coordinate dishware. Thankfully, Morocco's full array of pottery serves as ample inspiration, so that coordinating does not mean simply collecting all white dishes. Art is also integrated into tiny Moroccan kitchens in clever ways to add interest. The souks have a never-ending supply of curios, which are arranged in kitchen nooks and crannies. While minimalism is not the guiding principle here, neither is an unedited jumble of goods. Witty shelfscapes, careful layering, and dual-purpose objects are the name of the game.

Not surprisingly, the eat-in kitchen in medina houses is relatively rare, and, when found, is often limited to a space with a two-person café table. Frustrated with these constrictions, some riad and dar owners convert a larger room into a kitchen. It is also sometimes possible to knock down the wall between the kitchen and the neighboring room so as to allow for a dining table on one side and a kitchen on the other.

Left: The size of the kitchen in Catherine's Essaouira home is typical for a Moroccan riad. Catherine's cook, Fatima, finds everything conveniently within arm's reach. Arch-shaped cubbies store kitchen necessities, and a tagine waits on the stove to be used. Top: The Dar Rumi proprietors decorate their small riad-sized refrigerator with red hand of Fatima stickers, which can be bought in the souks. Above: Yann's pottery collection decorates the small kitchen of his Marrakesh flat, adding sculptural interest.

Like other rooms in riads and dars, these eat-in kitchens are typically long and narrow, requiring long and narrow tables to match. Ceilings tend to be very tall, presenting further decorating challenges.

Kitchens in newer villas are more spacious and light-filled. There is room for an island or a table in the middle and considerably more counter and cabinet space. There are usually multiple windows, and often there is a doorway leading outdoors, allowing for hot dishes to be easily carried to outside dining spaces. Additionally, villas offer more opportunities for eat-in kitchen seating arrangements, whether at freestanding tables or at built-in banquettes. Nonetheless, the open-plan kitchen that gives out onto the living room is rare in the Moroccan context, even in villas. The one exception to this rule is in newer modern apartments, where an occasional open-plan kitchen maximizes space and allows for ease of movement.

But no matter whether in a riad or a villa, Moroccan kitchens draw on artisanal inspiration and techniques. Counters are of polished cement in earthy colors, such as charcoal or chocolate; polished concrete is easy to maintain and naturally water-resistant. Alternatively,

Right: To provide for better flow, Natalie had a wall knocked down between her kitchen and her dining room, creating one long space. The dining table was custom made, with wooden stools used as seating. A vintage carpet is hung tapestry-style on the far wall. Fine Moroccan detailing can be seen in the original geps ceiling, the arched windows, and the doorway with its zellij tile. Opposite: Jamila prepares a meal in the kitchen in Natalie's Marrakesh riad. A no-nonsense affair, the kitchen features simple concrete shelving and no overhead cabinetry. With its ivory plaster walls, the black and white cement tiling provides the decorative element in the room. On the wall is a vintage star light fixture from the 1960s, found in the souks.

slick surfaces of Moroccan marble or granite can make an appearance, perfect for rolling out pastry. Kitchen cabinet doors are often composed of painted wood lattice strips or dowel-work mashrabiyas, which not only promote ventilation but also add texture. On walls, lustrous tadelakt finishes in natural shades complement the food. Meanwhile, on floors, tile adds bold style or quiet depth, depending on the coloring and the pattern. Tile can also be found winding its way up from the floor to the kitchen backsplash or be swapped out for zellij compositions that provide graphic interest and keep cooks stimulated. The whole look and feel of the Moroccan kitchen is cozy, warm, and handmade. It's a look that can be easily interpreted, too.

Above: In Rose's kitchen, the walls are a pale saffron tadelakt, the floors a neutral bejmat tile. Shelving is open, allowing cooks to help themselves to tagines, bowls, and spices in a flash. **Right:** *We chose a red, white, and black color story for our kitchen at Peacock Pavilions. A graphic statement is made with Popham Design cement tiles on the floor and the red lacquer cabinetry. Seating is banquette style, tucked into a nook overlooking the olive grove beyond. The table and chairs are vintage and were thrifted in the souks.*

moroccan-inspired kitchens

- **BUY A VARIETY OF DECORATIVE PLATES AND PLATTERS** to stack on shelves or mount on kitchen walls to add a pop of color. They come in handy when you need extra plates for guests.

- **PICK UP A MOROCCAN COOKING VESSEL**, the conical tagine, online or in the souks. Unglazed versions are suitable for food preparation, while more decorative versions are pretty for serving.

- **INSTALL BRIGHTLY PATTERNED CEMENT TILE** on the kitchen floor. The pattern will enliven your entire space and provide everyday inspiration for your cooking.

- **USE GLAZED ZELLIJ TILE** for a kitchen backsplash. The surface is not only beautiful but will make easy work of cleaning up oil splatters.

how to
MAKE MOROCCAN MINT TEA

Mint tea is not a mere drink in Morocco—it is a symbol of hospitality, friendship, and tradition. It's a ritual. No day is complete in Morocco without drinking multiple glasses, served both after meals and as a refreshment to accompany conversation. Poured from a fanciful metal teapot, tea is served in small, ornate tea glasses—plain, etched, or hand-painted with designs. Here is how to make the perfect glass.

INGREDIENTS

- **Green gunpowder tea**
- **Boiling water**
- **Handful of fresh mint leaves**
- **Sugar**

DIRECTIONS

1. Add a palmful of tea pellets to a teapot.

2. Pour a splash of boiling water over the tea and then pour the water out to rinse the tea, then repeat, in order to prevent bitterness and lighten the flavor.

3. Add to the teapot two handfuls of rinsed, fresh mint leaves on top of the rinsed gunpowder, along with sugar to taste.

4. Fill the teapot with boiling water.

5. Do not swirl or stir the tea, but rather infuse it through a ritual of pouring a glass and then pouring the glass back into the teapot, up to four times, to blend and cool the Moroccan "whiskey."

6. Serve immediately. Drink plain or add more sugar to taste.

NOTE: When drinking mint tea, it is traditional to have three glasses. In fact, a Moroccan proverb says, "The first glass is as bitter as life, the second glass is as sweet as love, the third glass is as gentle as death." So drink up.

Metallics add glamour to Anne's small
riad kitchen.

MOROCCAN FOOD AND MAGICAL BARAKA

Baraka is an important concept in Morocco and, more generally, in Islam. In its most basic sense, *baraka* is an Arabic word for divine or holy blessings and good luck. It is also used to express a genuine desire for the success and good fortune of others. In the Moroccan Darija dialect, *baraka* can refer to abundance and fulfillment, as well as to virtue and healing powers. Good deeds are thought to create baraka, and certain things are believed to intrinsically contain baraka. The Prophet Mohammed is thought to have had more baraka than anyone ever, some of which has been passed down to his descendants. Through their piety, saints also amass baraka.

Want to improve your luck? Try these foods, which some Moroccans believe will increase your baraka:

SAFFRON: Saffron is thought to inherently possess baraka and, if used, is believed to immerse the body in beneficial healing powers.

OLIVES: Olives are holy and associated with baraka in Islam; it is said that an olive tree has an invisible holy word written on each of its leaves.

MILK AND BUTTER: Milk and butter are thought to be charged with baraka, partially because the color white represents purity.

SALT: Salt has particularly strong baraka elements and is believed to ward off evil genies.

Bathrooms

Moroccan bathrooms are generally small. This is particularly true in traditional riads and dars in the medinas, where space is at a premium and where people traditionally take advantage of public baths, or hammams, for a leisurely steam and a weekly scrub.

Because medina bathrooms are so small, showers are generally preferred over tubs, and it is rare to have both in a bathroom. In many baths, there is little separation between the shower and the rest of the room; often, there will be a showerhead on one wall with a drain on the floor, and the sink and toilet will simply be to one side. Alternatively, there will be a partial shower enclosure, often structural in nature, made out of polished cement or tadelakt. Sometimes homeowners take the opportunity to carve these enclosures into arabesque shapes to add Moroccan architectural appeal. For those who feel constrained by the lack of space in the bath, renovation is always possible by knocking down a wall or two. And some will simply put a bathtub in a bedroom, in a modern open-plan style.

However, what Moroccan bathrooms may lack in size, they make up for with tactile materials and finishes, intriguing colors and patterns, and Moorish cabinetry and fittings. Upscale bathrooms are frequently found wrapped in glowing tadelakt surfaces, from floors to walls to ceilings; this creates a cocoonlike and sybaritic feel. Tadelakt has an inky and handmade appearance, adding to the sensual nature of the bathing experience. Alternatively, marble-tiled floors with white or black veins, or marble-clad showers or baths, can turn bathrooms into glamorous affairs. In a complete about-face, cheery tiles in bright shades can make bathing an upbeat experience. Glazed tile gleams and creates a jewelry box–like feel, while cement tile is matte and gives a subtle, soft glow. Along with color, Moroccan pattern can make a dramatic impact in bathrooms. A patterned cement tile can be used in small or large doses, adding dynamism. The tile can be limited to the floor, or run up the walls, giving bathers the impression that they are literally surrounded by pattern. Tile can also be laid with borders or plinths or in different combinations to add interest in these small spaces.

Opposite: The arch shaped opening to this curvy shower is a scene-stealer in Catherine's Essaouira riad. *Above, left:* A bedroom has been converted into a bath and dressing room in Natalie's riad. On the far end of the room is a silk-covered daybed, where Natalie likes to retreat to read. A gray-painted tea table is a convenient landing pad for books. *Above:* The vintage claw-foot tub was found in the Marrakesh souks. On the floor, a vintage carpet adds a splash. *Left:* The art deco dresser, also bought in the souks, houses Natalie's jewelry.

In addition to bold strokes in the bathroom, quieter touches can also make their mark, through cabinetry, linens, and other accessories. There are very few prefabricated bathroom vanities in Morocco. Instead, homeowners often build permanent vanities out of polished cement that blend seamlessly with the walls and the floors; these are smooth to the touch with soft corners. Alternatively, cabinetry draws on Moroccan shapes and textures for inspiration. There is a variety of artisanal sinks on offer, including clay ones with painted designs, as well as handmade sinks of brass, copper, or maillechort. Arched mirrors in horseshoe shapes are typical, as are those with inlaid designs. Unique accessories including cups, soap dishes, hammam bowls, and vintage pails make bathrooms feel gracious and homey.

In addition to the standard home bathroom, there is the hammam, the Moroccan version of the steam bath. (While the hammam is no stranger elsewhere in the Arab world, it is often associated with Morocco simply because the country has so many.) In addition to tony private hammams, public hammams are found in virtually every large neighborhood. Hammams have Islamic significance because the Prophet Muhammad liked hot baths and endorsed them, partly because they were thought to increase fertility. Hammams also provided the place and means to complete the cleansing rituals required before prayer. Going to the hammam was once seen as such a fundamental right that a husband's refusal to let his wife go regularly could be grounds for her initiating a divorce!

The hammam experience usually involves a soaking with pails of hot water, exfoliation with a kees (a coarse mitt), a lathering with sabon el beldi (an olive oil–based soft soap), and the application of rhassoul (a special clay mask).

*Opposite: Black tadelakt walls in Sylvain's bathroom in Essaouira give a minimalist cool to the space. He accessorizes with a hand-carved raw wood ladder. **Left:** Two types of arches are incorporated on John's mirror and vanity in his Essaouira apartment. Warm ivory tadelakt walls and two long slim Moroccan lanterns complete the look. **Below:** Helmut used orange- and lemon-colored glazed tile on the floors and walls to create an unforgettable bathroom. White racing stripes help structure the space.*

moroccan-inspired bathrooms

- **USE A HAMMAM BOWL** in your bathroom. Let it take the place of your soap dish or stash it in the shower to hold a razor in style.

- **SANDBLAST A MOROCCAN PATTERN** onto a window or a shower door for a stylized look. The pattern will also cast pretty shadows on the walls and floor.

- **HANG MOROCCAN GLASS LANTERNS** with clear panes on either side of your bathroom mirror. The exotic panache it provides will make your bath a place you will want to spend time in.

- **RUN A PATTERNED MOROCCAN CEMENT TILE** across your bathroom floor and all the way up your shower. The pattern will push out and expand the space.

how to

MAKE HAMMAM-WORTHY BEAUTY TREATMENTS

Living in the arid and sunny climate of Marrakesh is drying for hair and skin. I look to my own olive grove to whip up these simple beauty treatments, inspired by the indulgence of the hammam.

Olive Oil Hair Mask

This simple mask is nourishing for your hair and scalp and is particularly good for dry or chemically treated locks. Use it once or twice a month to provide an extra boost to your hair.

INGREDIENTS
- 3 tablespoons (45 ml) olive oil
- 1 whole egg

DIRECTIONS

1. In a small bowl, mix the oil and the egg.

2. Massage the mixture thoroughly into your hair, put on a shower cap, and wrap your head in a towel.

3. Relax for 20 minutes.

4. Shampoo twice, rinsing all of the mixture out of your hair. Style your hair as normal.

NOTE: You can also make this mask substituting 2 tablespoons (30 ml) of honey for the egg.

Olive Oil Face Mask

I am amazed by the goodness of olive oil, a gift of Morocco's most ubiquitous trees. Treat yourself to this homemade face mask about twice a month in winter.

INGREDIENTS
- 1 egg
- 1 tablespoon (15 ml) natural unbleached flour
- 1 tablespoon (15 ml) whole milk
- 1 teaspoon (5 ml) olive oil
- 1 teaspoon (5 ml) sea salt

DIRECTIONS

1. Whisk the egg in a small bowl.

2. Add the other ingredients one by one, stirring until completely mixed.

3. Apply the mask to your clean, dry face, and relax for 10 minutes.

4. Massage your face to gently exfoliate the skin and then rinse thoroughly. Gently pat dry.

Transitional Spaces: Entries, Hallways, and Stairs

Many Moroccan homes feature carefully chosen details in their transitional spaces, whether it's an entryway, a hallway, or a staircase. Centuries old, entries into riads and dars tend to be dark, with the only natural light coming from the front door. They habitually take the form of low-ceilinged, sunken hallways that make a sharp turn at the end, keeping the rest of the house entirely private. Flooring is typically decorative cement tile, which is hard-wearing and utilitarian and ideal for dusty shoes. The tile may extend one-third of the way up the walls, filling the space with exuberant pattern. Carpet runners or particularly easy-care rag rugs soften the floor's surface. Given the dearth of light, flat-bottomed lanterns are hung on either side of the hallway or placed on the steps. Additionally, there may be wall sconces or several pendant lights. Hooks, shelves, or foyer tables act as receptacles for all manner of items needed when coming and going.

*Right: In Catherine's hallway in her Essaouira riad, color and pattern abound. A vintage Moroccan carpet is layered over a checkerboard cement floor. The open pattern work of the mashrabiya chair is rivaled only by the ironwork of the railing overlooking the courtyard. **Opposite:** John's wide hallway in his Essaouira apartment is furnished like a room. Modern furniture and brightly colored lanterns are juxtaposed with a vintage carpet found in the souk. The arched window and doorway add Moroccan architectural appeal.*

Tagines are displayed like artwork in
Helmut's riad entry.

Patterned tile and colorful Moroccan rag
rugs liven up Natalie's foyer.

Closed hallways are relatively few in riads. Rather, covered walkways or galleries lead off the courtyard on the first floor or look down on the courtyard on the second and third floors. These walkways are generally airy and light and—if not too narrow—are often treated as additional living spaces. They can include seating in the form of chairs and poufs, as well as side tables on which to place glasses of mint tea and stacks of magazines. Floors are generally surfaced with glazed or cement tile, and carpet runners provide a comfortable landing for slippered feet. In villas, hallways are typically traditional and may be quite long. In keeping with Moroccan architectural style, arcaded hallways are not unusual and provide the perfect opportunity to showcase a long string of lanterns.

Staircases, particularly in riads, are also quite memorable. As many of these homes were built hundreds of years prior, staircases are frequently out of compliance with building codes; steps and risers are too short, and headroom is uncomfortably limited. Despite these constraints, old staircases feature a surprising display of color and pattern. Graphic printed tiles are ubiquitous along treads and run straight up the walls. In more upscale homes, intricate zellij is featured on the risers. Alternatively, walls and stairs may have a tadelakt finish in a saturated color, making the very act of walking up and down the stairs enjoyable. In newer villas, staircases tend to be more spacious, with adequate tread and headroom. In keeping with Moroccan tradition, these villa stairways are also viewed as opportunities for decoration. Color and pattern usually make themselves seen, often in astonishing ways.

Opposite: Oversized lanterns by
Ludovic Petit hang in Rose's hallway.
The curtains—orange and ivory hand-
guided machine embroidery on heavy
chocolate linen—were also designed
by Ludovic. *Right:* A heavy studded
door opens to Anne's riad entryway.
A Moroccan wedding chest provides
ample room to set down the day's
purchases from the souks. A vintage
carpet with talismanic symbols is
subtle artwork for the floor.

Two stairways at Peacock Pavilions were designed to showcase different Moroccan patterns. On the left, classic geometric patterns have been stenciled in shades of soft black and white. Melanie Royals of Royal Design Studio designed the stencils, which were used by visiting decorative artists under Melanie's tutelage. On the right, various Moroccan henna designs have been stenciled in shades of ivory and taupe. The treads are Moroccan marble, and the banister was designed by my husband.

moroccan-inspired entries, hallways, and stairs

- **HANG A SERIES OF MARKET BASKETS** on hooks in your entry. They're ideal for storing umbrellas, hats, and scarves so you can grab them on the go.

- **RUN A SUCCESSION OF PIERCED LANTERNS** down a long hallway. The patterns they cast will make your hallway feel like a destination itself.

- **PLACE ONE OR TWO VINTAGE MOROCCAN METALWARE CONTAINERS** on your entry table. Squirrel away mail, bills, and keys in these containers.

- **PLAY WITH COLOR OR PATTERN** on your stair risers. Try using graduated colors, for example, moving from pale yellow on the bottom step to deep saffron on the top one.

chapter 8

OUTDOOR LIVING SPACES AND GARDENS

One of the major advantages of living in Morocco is its sublime weather. With the exception of summer, the climate is temperate year-round in much of the country, and it is sunny nearly every day. Not surprisingly, people spend a great deal of time in the open air, whether they live in riads in the medinas or in villas in the new cities. Thus, outdoor spaces and gardens are treated like important additional living spaces and are decorated accordingly.

Outdoor Living Spaces

Moroccan homes are designed to maximize outdoor living space with roof terraces, verandas, porches, and patios that blur the distinctions between outside and inside. And since outdoor dining is possible three seasons a year, almost every Moroccan home has at least one furnished outdoor area just for this purpose. Alfresco dining is truly one of life's daily pleasures in Morocco.

ROOF TERRACES

Most villas and riads have handy flat roof terraces. For villas, a roof terrace offers a different perspective overlooking the grounds and gardens. Villa roof terraces are also wonderful settings from which to watch sunsets. For riads, rooftop terraces function as critical outdoor rooms and often contain more than one corner for living and dining. These spaces are naturally partitioned by the interior courtyard, creating several semiprivate zones. In addition to areas in which to eat and lounge, there may be rooftop kitchens and outdoor showers, as well as places to hang laundry to dry. With high parapet walls, these spaces are usually quite concealed, and strict building codes help ensure that neighbors are not privy to the goings-on of others. Occasionally, there is more than one level to rooftops, with staircases leading up to a small section with particularly privileged views. These spots feel almost nestlike and are perfect for catching a breeze on a hot summer night and enjoying a cool drink under the stars.

Rooftop seating areas, particularly in riads, are frequently of the built-in variety, designed to fully exploit precious outdoor space. Similar to banquettes in living rooms, this seating is made out of wood, or sometimes cement, ensuring that the structure is permanently affixed. Rattan and wicker furniture and

butterfly chairs made from canvas are also popular. Given Morocco's strong sun, particularly in higher elevations, seating and dining areas are usually covered at a minimum by umbrellas. These umbrellas are often of the oversized variety, providing shelter for two or more people. More protection may be provided by large tarps made out of unbleached canvas, creating a tentlike structure. Alternatively, rattan or slatted roofs cast pretty shadows and offer at least partial protection. Potted plants abound, bringing greenery to the roof. It's typical for rugs to be unfurled on a roof for an evening dinner party and lanterns scattered in corners to add glow and magic.

Previous pages, left: On Natalie's riad rooftop terrace, breakfast is served at a wooden table, faded to a pale gray from the Moroccan sun. A minimal lattice roof casts intriguing shadows at midday. The potted plants help fashion a verdant getaway in the midst of the medina. Previous pages, right: Natalie's rooftop terrace offers different spots for different purposes. Here, a seating area provides a quiet place for her to recover after a day at her Marrakesh photography gallery. The uncomplicated furnishings were thrifted in the souks. The apple is a remnant of an Adam and Eve–themed soiree in Paris that Natalie organized for Cartier, where she formerly worked. Opposite: A row of small Moroccan lanterns provides magical lighting for dinners with friends on the roof terrace of Anne's Marrakesh riad. Guests can lounge on banquette seating covered with multihued cushions. Left: A private corner of Sylvain's rooftop terrace provides a sunny location for an outdoor shower.

VERANDAS AND PORCHES

Villas habitually include arcaded verandas that run the entire length of the back of the house, giving out onto the private garden. These fully furnished spaces are often covered by cement roofs to ensure total protection from the sun and the rain. When such permanent roofing is not available, slatted roofs will do double duty as trellises. Here flowering vines will be coaxed to grow, providing fragrance and color and blocking the sun's rays. A series of lanterns characteristically hangs overhead, running the full course of the porch or veranda. Wicker pendant lighting—handmade in the souks—is also typical. Tall curtains are sometimes installed in the arcades, allowing homeowners to draw them when the sun is too strong.

Zellij tables are ubiquitous in ground-floor outdoor areas, as they hold up to the elements with ease and are long-wearing. These zellij tables come in a wide range of colors and designs. Homeowners can choose a stark and modern look with a monochrome tile, or opt for a traditional look, with a plain center and a contrasting border. Alternatively, tables featuring complex geometric tile patterns in two, three, or more shades show off Moroccan craftsmanship with flair. For the sake of portability, café tables are also common, allowing tables to be regrouped with ease to accommodate different combinations of guests. These tables are typical of Morocco's French café culture, where people linger with friends over cups of nouss-nouss (café au lait) or glasses of mint tea. Sometimes large, low tea tables—inexpensive and practical—are seen, too, reproducing the feel of Moroccan salons. Plain wooden farm tables are occasionally found as well. Tables are paired with painted rattan chairs, country chairs made with unvarnished wood, or molded plastic chairs—a throwback to Morocco's more bohemian era.

Lounging areas are usually of the banquette variety, although sometimes a back will be added to allow the piece to be freestanding. In general, fully upholstered seating is not uncommon outdoors, particularly when there is a roof overhead ensuring that the furniture is protected. Given that there is relatively little rain in many areas of Morocco, some people simply don't worry about potential raindrops and create fully decorated outdoor rooms, complete with carpets. Furnishings can always be covered and rugs taken in on those rare instances when the weather takes a turn for the worse.

Outdoor flooring is often blanketed with bejmat or cement tile in colors reminiscent of the earth, blending in with the landscape. Then again, some homeowners opt for a more upbeat mood with glazed tile in bright shades of blue or green, laid in fun patterns. For a look that is industrial, warm, or glamorous, depending on the color and design, dess flooring is also a slick and durable option for the outdoors.

Corinne styled an outdoor seating area with indoor furnishings from her Marrakesh shop, Lilah Spirit. Outfitting a patio with "real furniture" makes spending time outdoors so much more comfortable.

Hosting a lunch outside with guests seated
on sequined handwoven cushions is so Moroccan.

Shadows thrown from Moroccan doors and
Trellises provide the artwork on this patio.

Left: Photographer Delphine Warin's porch is the coziest place in the house. Simple banquette seating is loaded with geometric-patterned textiles and vintage cushions. Two tea tables—one low and one high—can be pulled up for easy access to drinks and snacks. A color-paned lantern provides pretty lighting. *Above:* Plants and trees provide a beautiful backdrop for breakfast on the veranda of Corinne's Marrakesh villa. It's an idyllic spot to start to the day.

FREESTANDING HARDSCAPED AND OTHER SPACES

Some fortunate villa owners also have detached, fully hardscaped outdoor rooms, especially if the gardens are extensive. These take the shape of fanciful domed pergolas made out of wrought iron with seating below, or discreet structures made out of slatted wood or branches that allow for reading or lunching in a quiet, natural setting. Moroccan tents are also common. These tents are not typically meant for sleeping (although many guesthouses now offer that option) but rather for dining or lounging. Rustic peaked Berber tents are usually made of brown, rough-hewn blanket material and decorated with brightly colored pom-poms and woven straps. These Berber tents are permanently open on one side, propped up by wooden poles, and staked to the ground. Inside, you can find carpets, poufs, and low tea tables. Arabian-styled white tents are another outdoor space option. These are often airy, large structures made out of fabric, with windows and doors that roll up and down and walls that may be drawn like curtains. Such tents are usually permanent structures placed on a cement slab and wired for electricity. A series of banquettes along with round tables or freestanding tables and chairs can be found inside. Carpets or tiling is standard for the floor, and lanterns are usually hung overhead.

*Right: Geraldine and David's villa on the grounds of the Beldi Country Club has one of Marrakesh's loveliest gardens. Everywhere you turn there are spaces to enjoy the beautiful scenery. Geraldine and David created this simple pergola so that they can enjoy lunches in the shade surrounded by climbing flowering vines. **Following pages:** The dining tent at Peacock Pavilions is an ode to Moroccan textiles. The tent itself was made by local tentmakers. The walls were stenciled with Fez embroidery designs using stencils commissioned from Melanie Royals of Royal Design Studio. The painting was executed by Melanie and a group of painters. On the floor is a collection of vintage carpets. Moroccan wedding blankets cover the low seating.*

POOLS AND FOUNTAINS

Given the weather, swimming is possible for a good part of the year in Morocco. In riads, pools are most often found in the center of courtyards, although they are occasionally seen on rooftop terraces. In villas, the opportunities multiply given the more ample lawns and gardens. Pool designs range from plain to fanciful, with some pools mimicking the shape of a Moroccan arch. In addition to glass tile, pools may have tadelakt surfaces, which are naturally resistant to water. Glazed bejmat tiling is also used. Adjoining pool cabanas allow swimmers to read, write, or just relax outside without worrying about the sun's harsh rays. And sun loungers are dotted here and there, havens for those who want to work on their tans or dry off after dips in the pool. Large umbrellas are a must and provide a certain architectural structure to pool areas.

In keeping with Islamic tradition, pretty fountains, basins, and waterways are also habitually a part of the landscaping, valued for their beauty alone. These are used strategically: Small fountains might line the path to the main door, as is the case at Peacock Pavilions; or a low basin with a discreet spout might be the center of a walkway roundabout; or a waterway might connect one part of the garden to another.

Opposite: The pool at Peacock Pavilions is located in an outdoor courtyard with an open-air trellised cabana on one end. Left: The pool in Alessandro's Marrakesh riad is covered with rose petals—a poetic way to greet guests.

moroccan-inspired outdoor living spaces

- **LINE BOTH SIDES OF YOUR FRONT PATH** with lanterns. They will enchant your guests and create an exotic ambiance when people walk to your front door.

- **MAKE AN OUTDOOR BANQUETTE** out of wood pallets and a twin mattress. Throw a pretty coverlet and multiple pillows on top for a bohemian place to lounge on your porch.

- **SPLURGE ON A FOUNTAIN** to turn your outdoor space into a Moroccan retreat. If hooking up a fountain seems daunting, a simple large basin will do. Fill it with rose petals or even whole roses.

- **TAKE THREE OR FOUR CARPETS OUTSIDE**, as well as low tables and cushions, and throw an evening lawn party. String up inexpensive lanterns in the trees to complete the ambiance.

Gardens

Gardens, big or small, are vital in Morocco. Since much of Morocco is arid or semiarid, gardeners work within some tricky constraints. Given the limited rainfall in many parts of the country, drought-resistant plants do best. Plants also need to be hardy—resistant to both dry heat by day and in summer, and desert cold by night and in winter. Despite these limitations, there is a wide variety of trees, flowering plants, succulents, cacti, and herbs in Morocco.

TREES

Morocco is famous for its palm groves, which stretch like a shaggy jungle in certain parts of the country, including Marrakesh. Although there are several kinds of palms available, only two species are native to Morocco—doum palms and date palms (and here's an odd fact: only "female" palms have dates). Palms are especially coveted for lining villa driveways and walkways, giving instant volume and drama. Although these are hardy trees, they can suffer if not transplanted with proper care.

Citrus trees are plentiful, especially orange, tangerine, and lemon trees. Most citrus trees were introduced to Morocco as early as the thirteenth century. Mandarin orange trees with their shiny leaves and sculptural form are a striking choice and are routinely

seen in sidewalk gardens. Other fruit trees, including fig, pomegranate, peach, apricot, plum, and apple, and bushes are abundantly incorporated in landscaping around villas. Pear trees can also be found, as can walnut trees and almond trees, both native to Morocco.

Beyond fruit trees, Morocco is well known for its olive groves, which is why there are so many, many Moroccan recipes calling for olives and olive oil. Olive trees are believed to be the most indigenous of all Moroccan trees—dating back to well before the Arab conquest. With the trees' silvery leaves, the groves appear to shimmer when a breeze blows. Flowering trees such as jacaranda (introduced by the French) and pepper trees (introduced by the Spanish) can also be found in gardens. Pine, fir, and cypress trees were all introduced to Morocco centuries ago and are often used as green barriers surrounding properties. These trees are particularly sculptural and are used wherever a little drama is needed.

SUCCULENTS AND CACTI

Environmentally friendly succulents are widely available for purchase in Morocco. The euphorbia is native to Morocco, but most others, including the agaves, are originally from North America (introduced by the Spanish). These plants need minimal care and flourish on rooftops and gardens. Desert-loving cacti, too, are widespread. With their spiky leaves, cacti are often planted as natural barricades around villas—dissuasive to all but the most determined intruders. A side benefit is artistic-looking cactus fruit. These plants do well planted in pots or in the ground, making them a go-to plant for many homeowners.

Previous page, left: Citrus trees are omnipresent in parks throughout Morocco. Previous page, right: Layers of plants, vines, shrubs, and trees greet visitors at the entrance of Geraldine and David's Marrakesh villa. Opposite: Majestic cypress trees punctuate the walkway to the front door of Stephanie's Marrakesh villa. The look is crisp and structured. Right: In a corner of his rooftop terrace in Essaouira, Sylvain has created a modernist spot to sunbathe. The succulents and cacti hit all the right notes.

FLOWERING PLANTS

Much of Morocco is in bloom for substantial parts of the year. In classic Mediterranean style, flowering vines are omnipresent, dripping off balconies, climbing up walls, and hanging from pergolas. Vine varieties include native honeysuckle, bougainvillea (in pinks, reds, yellows, violets, and white), and jasmine. Roses, too, are ubiquitous and make up much of the flower market's offerings. These bloom in the hundreds in gardens all over the country. It's no wonder that Morocco is a rose-exporting country and that rose products, including rose cream and rose soap, fill Moroccan apothecaries. Hardy rose types include *Rosa × damascena*, with its pink flower—used in the Moroccan spice mixture ras el hanout and to make rose water for flavoring desserts. Native oleander is another widespread flowering plant.

Right: Bougainvillea climbs over trellises and entries at Peacock Pavilions, providing a welcome element of freshness. Their color is striking all year round. Opposite: Hundreds of white rose bushes bloom at Peacock Pavilions. The property's fifty-year-old olive trees—laid out in a tidy grid—stand like sentries guarding the roses.

HERBS

Morocco is a spicy country, literally and figuratively. So it makes sense that herbs play an important role in gardens, as many find their way into simmering Moroccan tagines. There is an abundance of aromatic varieties on offer, including several that are native to Morocco, such as rosemary, thyme, oregano, coriander, and lavender. More recently introduced, bay, cumin, and parsley are popular in Moroccan kitchens. Rosemary is often grown into delicious-smelling hedges, while several varieties of mint grow invasively and can be found daily in pots of fresh tea in Moroccan homes.

Hedging at Peacock Pavilions is made of rosemary that was grown from seedlings. Incredibly hardy and fast growing, this fragrant plant has so many uses in the kitchen.

moroccan gardens

- **TRAIN BOUGAINVILLEA TO CLIMB ONTO TRELLISES** abutting dining areas in your backyard or grow jasmine over your front doorway. In an apartment, layer cascading vines along with other plants in your window boxes.

- **GROW A PATCH OF MINT,** which will come in handy when making Moroccan mint tea. In an apartment, placing a small potted mint plant in a sunny spot on a kitchen window will add fragrance.

- **PLANT A SUCCULENT CARPET** in a small area of your backyard using multiple clusters of identical plants. Or vary the type, color, and height of plant to provide depth and interest.

- **CLUSTER PINK ROSEBUSHES OR SUCCULENTS** in pots on the steps of your front porch. Paint the pots Majorelle blue. This dose of lively color will be therapy for you and your guests.

how to

CREATE A MOROCCAN HERB GARDEN

In a Moroccan–French fusion, create an herb garden that is as useful as it is lovely. The traditional French pattern for an herb garden is a square divided into four squares, or parterres, separated by two paths that intersect in the middle. The squares are then lined with a type of shrub to define each space, and herbs and other ornamental flowers or trees are planted within the squares. You can, however, choose from any number of designs or create your own design using circles, squares, or other arabesque patterns. For our garden at Peacock Pavilions, we further subdivided the four major squares by halving or quartering them to provide extra visual and herbal variety.

MATERIALS

- **String**
- **2 wooden markers or stakes**
- **Shrubs, for hedging, such as rosemary**
- **Herb plants, such as mint, parsley, coriander, thyme, basil, verbena, sage, etc. The number you need depends on the size of your space.**
- **Gardening trowel or shovel**

DIRECTIONS

1. Using string wound between two stakes, mark out where you want your herb garden to be. If you have an existing path or intersecting paths, you may create the herb garden with those paths marking your way. If you are creating a circular design, mark out a perfect circle by placing one stake in the ground at the center of your space and, with a length of string and another stake on the opposite end, make one revolution around your center stake. Score the ground where your shrubs will be planted.

2. Plant your shrubs for hedging about 1 foot (30 cm) apart. As the hedge grows, it will fill out, and you can shape it as you wish.

3. Within each section of your herb garden, plant a different herb, massing them for effect.

4. Add decorative plants in touches according to your taste. You might consider rose topiaries or citrus trees in the center of each parterre, for example. Not only does this give a garden some height, but it also adds a different color. You can decide on any number of variations to your garden.

5. To maintain your garden, water, weed, and fertilize. Enjoy your fresh herbs and flowers.

PART III

Sourcing Moroccan Style

All of Morocco's major cities are home to the famed souks, located in the medina on the bustling, narrow, winding streets and holding a wide array of treasures. The souks are typically organized by trade, such as the carpet souk, the leather souk, the metalworkers' souk, and so forth. For those who admire beauty and are attracted to the handmade, the souks are fascinating places. The spectrum of goods for sale is a feast for the eyes. Stylish boutiques in the new cities also offer particularly finely designed items, often with a more modern flair. Given all the treasures for sale, it is no surprise to learn that artisans make up nearly 20 percent of Morocco's workforce. Now that you've had some Moroccan style inspiration, this part is designed to give you a start on resourcing your own home with the very best Moroccan items. It includes two chapters that provide suggestions for what to buy and where to shop.

chapter 9

SHOPPING FOR CHIC

There are many special things to buy that will add Moroccan style to your home, from large pieces such as doors and furniture to small accessories like tea glasses and pottery. And you can never go wrong with investment pieces such as carpets and lighting. All of these elements, large or small, expensive or a bargain, will help provide your place with some Moroccan magic. Here are some of my favorite picks.

214

Carpets and Rugs

Moroccan rugs are very popular on the global decorating scene. Styles range dramatically, as do prices. Most Moroccan carpets are made of sheeps' or goats' wool, although some are made of cotton, silk, goat hair, camel hair, leather, palm reeds, and even old clothes. (Technically, "wool" is the soft part of animal hair, and "hair" is made up of coarser wool strands.) Good-quality wool has a sheen to it, which happens only if the animal is alive when sheared. Accordingly, "live wool" is more expensive than "dead wool" and is not only more lustrous, but also less brittle. Cotton—far less expensive than wool—is becoming increasingly popular in Moroccan rugs.

Moroccan carpets are often referred to by the city or area where they were made or by the tribe that made them. While each area or tribe has distinctive carpet styles, no two carpets are ever exactly alike, as they are handmade. More generally, carpets can be loosely divided into two categories: urban and rural. Urban rugs tend to be more refined and reminiscent of Persian or Ottoman designs; they can be recognized by single or multiple central medallions, symmetrical patterns with arabesques and floral features, and clearly delineated borders. These carpets typically have a higher knot count than their rural counterparts and are often less shaggy. Historically, Moroccan urban rugs have been produced in workshops and small craft collectives.

Rural rugs are made by women from Berber or Arab tribes, normally in the home (although women's carpet-producing cooperatives have cropped up in rural areas, too). Coveted in the interior design world for years, rural Moroccan rugs tend to feature simpler straight lines and may have abstract patterns or talismanic symbols. The carpet weft can be irregular and is generally not tight, and the rugs are often asymmetrical. They can be found in pile or flat-weave versions, woven from wool or sometimes cotton, goat hair, or even camel hair. Additionally, boucherouite (rag rugs made from strips of old clothing) are turning up around the country.

TIPS FOR BUYING MOROCCAN CARPETS AND RUGS

AGE: You won't find Moroccan rugs more than a hundred years old—those are considered antiques and are in rare supply. Chemical dyes have been used by Moroccan weavers since the late 1800s, so vivid colors are not a good indication of a rug's age.

BARGAINING: Moroccan carpet dealers tend to have notoriously large markups on their carpets. So make sure to bargain hard—offer one-quarter to one-third of the asking price and go from there.

CERTIFICATION: Moroccan government–certified rugs must be knotted, handmade, and all wool; they can be found at Moroccan government cooperative stores. But don't miss amazing rug bargains—especially beautiful vintage pieces—in the souks.

COLORFASTNESS: Make sure rug dyes are colorfast. You can test this by wetting a napkin and pressing it against the rug; if the napkin stays white, the dyes are colorfast. (Poor-quality reds are especially prone to bleeding.)

GUIDES: Beware of carpet shopping with guides, who normally take significant kickbacks from carpet merchants. You are better off shopping alone.

UNDERSTANDING SYMBOLS ON YOUR MOROCCAN RUGS

Symbols are a common feature on rugs, adding mystery and talismanic intrigue. While many debate the precise meanings of these symbols, a few common ideas have held.

BEE: family happiness

BIRD: go-between for heaven and earth

CHEVRON: spread legs; fertility

CIRCLE: the full moon

DIAMOND: a mirror or an eye, for protection against the evil eye

FLOWERS: fertility

HAND: protection against the evil eye; can be realistically or abstractly depicted (for example, five dots or five lines)

LIZARD: human soul seeking the light

NESTED DIAMONDS: motherhood

SERIES OF TRIANGLES: the four seasons

SNAKE OR CROOKED LINE: fertility

TREE: happiness and fertility

TRIANGLE: a mirror or a stylized eye or hand, intended to protect people from the evil eye

VERTICAL CHAINS OF DIAMONDS: birth

X: scissors, for protection against the evil eye

ZIGZAG: a saw or a sickle, seen as protection from the evil eye (pointy and made of metal and therefore capable of bursting the evil eye)

Sometimes symbols in carpets are cut off at the ends without being completed, an occurrence that some experts refer to as "infinite rapport," whereby the carpet shows only part of the design but the design continues in the imagination infinitely.

Doors and Windows

Moroccan doors are decidedly famous because of their architectural shapes and intricate detailing. Although many of the exquisite antique doors were snapped up long ago, antique, vintage, and new doors can still be found. Some tower at twelve feet tall, and even the door handles have vertigo, screwed in at six feet off the ground. In terms of pattern, Moroccan doors are often quite decorative. Six- and eight-pointed stars and medallions feature heavily in painted and carved door designs. Rural Berber doors, with their multiple motifs—triangles, zigzags, concentric circles, and leaf shapes—are particularly charming. Rivets and interesting large brackets often provide a touch of metallic style in a sea of wood. Meanwhile, novelty comes from the smaller door-within-a-door versions.

Moroccan windows are also readily spotted in the souks, particularly lovely vintage ones. Most are bifurcated in the middle, shutter-style, and made out of wood with raised panels. Many have beautiful decorative metal grilles in the interior, with lacy scroll-like designs. Given their age, quite a few vintage Moroccan windows have remnants of paint, a reminder of their history and the whims of their previous owners.

TIPS FOR BUYING MOROCCAN DOORS AND WINDOWS

AUTHENTICITY: Antique doors are relatively rare and expensive, ranging from hundreds to thousands of dollars. Be wary of dealers selling "antique" doors that are suspiciously cheap.

SHIPPING: Doors tend to be heavy and large. Before you purchase one, calculate shipping costs based not only on weight, but also on volume.

USE: Many doors and windows, whether new or old, have small gaps in their joinery. Accordingly, they are better suited for use inside.

WOOD AGING: New wood in Morocco is not always properly aged before it's used. Check any doors and windows carefully for cracks and leaking of sap.

Door Knockers and Home Hardware

Moroccan doors are often embellished with a wide array of knockers and handles. A popular choice is the khamsa, or hand of Fatima, which is meant to ward off the evil eye. Mischievous genies are believed to hang out in doorways, making a khamsa door knocker an inexpensive deterrent. Other Moroccan door knockers include large circular lacy forms, stars, and geometric shapes, their brass forms cut out or etched with Islamic designs.

In addition to door knockers, there is an impressive variety of Moroccan–style hooks, brackets, handles, knobs, pulls, and even toilet paper holders and toilet brushes. These often have intricate hand-etching or cast Moroccan patterning. There are copper and brass sinks, as well as taps on offer, should a little artisanal splendor be called for in the bathroom. Decorative spouts for the ubiquitous Moroccan fountains can also be purchased, some in pretty petaled flower shapes.

TIPS FOR BUYING MOROCCAN DOOR KNOCKERS AND HARDWARE

CHINESE IMPORTS: Chinese versions of Moroccan hardware have invaded the marketplace and are not always high-quality. Ask pointedly if the item is made in Morocco before buying, as there are no telltale markings, such as MADE IN CHINA or MADE IN MOROCCO stamps.

TARNISHING: Brass and copper sinks tarnish quickly, especially as they are so regularly in contact with water. Avoid them unless you are committed to performing the extra maintenance.

DETAILING: Some hardware has crude designs and finishes. Run your hands over the whole item to check for rough edges and examine closely for workmanship.

AGING: Shiny brass can be aged on the spot with a chemical treatment. Many Moroccan hardware stores will do this for you for free upon request.

Furniture

Moroccan vendors carry the same assortment of basic furniture as vendors in many other countries, but a few pieces are notable because of their clear association with the country—namely, banquettes and tea tables. Moroccan wedding chests are less known but are very pretty, too. Furniture is typically made out of cedar, beech, thuya, walnut, and pine.

Moroccan tea tables have taken the design world by storm, and with good reason. They are light, portable, and practical, and often used in multiples. Tea tables are rarely square but rather are round, six- or eight-sided, or occasionally rectangular. The ornate carpentry of the banquette is sometimes replicated in the table, helping to tie the two items together. Tea tables typically have arches going around the sides and frequently come painted with elaborate floral motifs. Sometimes they come in two parts: a metal tray and a folding wood base.

Moroccan marriage or wedding chests harken back to a time when Berber brides would pack their belongings in this decorative piece of furniture. They are most often made of cedar and painted with astral motifs, horseshoe forms, and concentric circles in reds, greens, and ochres. Antique chests are hard to find these days, but good reproductions can still be seen in the Moroccan marketplace.

TIPS FOR BUYING MOROCCAN FURNITURE

PARTIAL BANQUETTE: Banquettes are large, heavy pieces and include significant amounts of plain, untreated wood (namely, the area where the mattress is intended to be placed). If weight/shipping is an issue, you may be better off purchasing only the decorative front piece of the banquette and making (or having someone else make) the rest at home.

PORTABILITY: Most tea tables can substitute in size for a piece of luggage on the plane but need to be wrapped in Bubble Wrap and boxed. Those tables made from a tray and a folding base can simply be placed in a suitcase, along with other items.

CRACKING: As wood is often not aged adequately in Morocco, cracking does occur. Check each piece carefully before you purchase it, making sure to look at the underside of the table, as well.

FINISH: Sometimes wood is not finely sanded before decorative painting occurs. Make sure the finish is smooth.

Lighting

The selection of Moroccan light fixtures is guaranteed to amaze. When it comes to lanterns, there's something for everybody, no matter what your taste or budget. One of the most important things to understand about Moroccan lighting is that the actual light emitted is secondary to the ambiance produced. In other words, the illumination is less important than the shadows. This is moody, romantic lighting at its very best.

In terms of styles of Moroccan light fixtures, there's a wide range: from the classic flat-bottomed lantern meant to be carried or to rest on the floor, to Arabian-style pendant lanterns with pointed metal bottoms intended to dangle from the ceiling, to sconces, in multiple sizes, for fastening directly to the wall. As for materials and price, there's a gamut from the fun tin sconce made from recycled cans to the carved bronze pendant light that requires weeks of work to make. Moroccan light fixtures made out of tin, brass, copper, bronze, animal skin, or fabric—or made with glass panes—are all worth a look.

TIN: The beauty of Moroccan tin lanterns lies in the fact that they are produced by a person, not a machine. Despite their humble material, they are pierced by hand and cast beautiful patterns all over floors, walls, and ceilings. Many are in the ubiquitous *Arabian Nights* styles, while others have more modern forms, such as balls.

BRASS, COPPER, AND BRONZE: The upper echelons of Moroccan lighting are made with nobler and heavier-grade metals, such as brass, copper, and bronze. These often feature intricate patterns, from rhythmic designs to sophisticated vines and flowers. However, far more important than the materials is the workmanship itself. Marrakesh is known for its fine metal hand-piercing with a chisel and a hammer, while in Fez the piercing is done with a tiny saw blade.

GLASS-PANED: Glass panes are common in Moroccan lanterns. These are either clear to allow for maximum light, or colored for a more festive look. Multiple colored panes on the same lantern are not unusual, typically a combination of blue, green, red, and yellow. These cast happy colored streams of light. Sometimes, the panes are made out of pressed glass, adding another layer of pattern and texture.

ANIMAL SKINS AND FABRIC: Animal skins and fabrics are stretched over metal frames in some Moroccan light fixtures. Undyed, the skins are thin and translucent in the light and are often used as the base for hand-painted henna designs. In a more modern twist, some designers incorporate fabrics into lighting, resulting in delicate creations that are hand-embroidered with floss, sequins, beads, or crystals.

TIPS FOR BUYING MOROCCAN LIGHTING

IMPERFECTIONS: While the handmade nature of lighting adds tremendous charm and a one-of-a-kind quality, it also means there may be imperfections. Check all sides of the lighting fixture for flaws, making sure that glass pieces are uncracked and metal parts undented.

WIRING: Most Moroccan lanterns come with no wiring at all. Buy the cord and a lightbulb at your local hardware store when you get home.

SHIPPING: All lanterns with glass parts are best hand-carried or shipped in a wooden crate by an expeditor. More expensive bronze, brass, and copper lanterns have a much higher chance of arriving in one piece than do thin metal or tin lanterns, which are easily dented.

Coloring: Moroccan lanterns with colored panes are not always colorfast, as the hues can fade when exposed to heat and light over the long haul. Although more expensive, fixtures with panes made out of what is known as Iraqi glass are far more reliable.

Henna: Henna designs painted on animal skin lanterns may not fare well over a period of years. The henna has a tendency to flake off, leaving patchy areas.

Market Baskets

Market baskets jostle for position in Moroccan souk stalls. These are not mere shopping fodder, but necessary accessories for those wishing to carry hefty loads of fresh fruit and vegetables from the market. Shopping baskets take many shapes and sizes—from petite to extra large. Many are made out of natural raffia, while others are colored, from yellow to purple to green (and every shade in between). Some boast leather handles and trim, embroidery in yarn, vintage fabrics, or shiny sequins. Newer models include those made with Moroccan plastic grain sacks or other recycled materials. Nearly all options are practical, fun, and affordable, and they make great gifts.

TIPS FOR BUYING MOROCCAN MARKET BASKETS

PACKING: Many market baskets—particularly those with more rigid frames—don't pack well. Use one as hand luggage on the plane or pack it into a large hardshell suitcase.

LEATHER TRIM: Be forewarned that leather handles on market baskets that are not brown may run on your hands. Check to see if dyes are colorfast.

SEQUINS: Not all sequined market baskets are created equal; some have plastic sequins sewn on by machine, while others have metal sequins sewn on by hand. Take a close look at potential purchases and shop accordingly.

GIFTS: If buying for friends and family, consider buying market baskets in sizes that nest in one another. This will mean one tidy parcel, rather than several.

Metalware

Moroccan vendors have a huge range of decorative metalware on offer, both new and vintage. Metalware may be aluminum, nickel, silver plated, maillechort, brass, or copper. Traditionally, metalware was finely engraved, stamped, or made with a repoussé technique. These days, modern hammered styles are also popular. As with many of the Moroccan arts, Fez is the hub of production for these items, but Marrakesh also has a very healthy selection in the souks.

Some options include:

BOXES: Boxes are often sold in sets of three and are available in round or oval shapes. They were traditionally made to store mint, tea, and sugar on a tea tray, but are also a pretty way to store jewelry and other treasures.

BREAD OR COOKIE HOLDERS: These two-piece containers feature high-peaked tops and short legs. In addition to providing an Orientalist way to serve baked goods,

they are useful for storing a variety of small items, from mail to keys.

INCENSE HOLDERS: The beauty of incense holders is the cutouts that allow the scent to dissipate. In addition to incense, I like to put votive candles in mine.

HAMMAM BOWLS: These bowls are traditionally used to ladle steaming water at the hammams (steam baths). They are generally made out of maillechort or brass and have delicate patterns etched on the bottom.

HAND WASHERS WITH PITCHERS: These decorative portable sinks have a built-in drainage system and handles to allow them to be carried easily. They are offered to guests to wash their hands.

PAILS: Metal pails are often covered in ornate floral designs and come in two sizes: large and small. They are most commonly used as dustbins but are also handy for all sorts of jobs; try one as a container for a potted plant or as an ice bucket for chilling wine.

PERFUME BOTTLES: These lovely bottles include intricate metal accents and are often used to sprinkle orange flower or rose water on hands. Sometimes they are made of vintage perfume bottles.

TEAPOTS: Morocco's ubiquitous teapots are used to serve steaming hot fresh mint tea. These teapots come in many styles and sometimes have a little bird or a colored finial on top.

TRAYS: Trays are available in a large variety of appealing shapes, including flowers, ovals, rounds, and rectangles. Sometimes trays come with low sides to securely hold glasses, teapots, and other accoutrements within.

WATER AND WINE BOTTLE HOLDERS: Slip your bottles right into these decorative holders to dress up their presentation for a lunch or a dinner. The holders, always manufactured new, are typically made to fit over the bottoms of large bottles of mineral water but can occasionally be found for wine bottles, too.

TIPS FOR BUYING MOROCCAN METALWARE

MAILLECHORT: Maillechort is undoubtedly the most tarnish-free of all metals on the Moroccan marketplace, and you will pay accordingly. If you are not a fan of polishing, be sure to ask vendors if your piece is maillechort.

LEGS: Many large trays actually have screw-on legs that allow your tray to sit up high. Flip a tray over to see if there are telltale holes, and if so, ask the vendor for the corresponding legs.

MATCHING: The matching tops of boxes and cookie holders sometimes go missing and are replaced with others. Examine the tops and bottoms of your items to see if they are meant to go together.

BOWLS: Some "hammam bowls" are actually domed lids of boxes. Make sure that your bowl sits perfectly flat and is balanced.

Mirrors

Many Moroccan mirror sellers display their wares on the street, offering numerous options that are ideal for a bedroom, a bathroom, or a hallway. Mirrors come in every size, from tiny palm-sized mirrors to tall and wardrobe-sized. Some are plain, but the majority of Moroccan mirrors are decorative, meant to be statement pieces.

The kitschiest mirrors are those made from recycled metal, displaying tomatoes or sardines. Then there are the mirrors made from old rubber tires, sometimes cut into oval or round shapes, or even into flowers, their material conveying a green version of cool. More upscale mirrors are made out of maillechort, copper, or brass, which is hammered, stamped, or engraved. Wood versions are often elaborately carved with arabesques or calligraphy or may be entirely hand-painted with delicate floral patterns, buds, and vines intertwining around the borders. Camel bone is occasionally embedded around a mirror's edge, reminding the buyer of the mirror's provenance. Additionally, numerous mirrors look like scaled-down versions of Moroccan city gates, shaped to emulate the rounded, horseshoe, and cusped arches of the entrances to the medina.

TIPS FOR BUYING MOROCCAN MIRRORS

EMBEDDED BONE: Whether in their natural white or a henna-dyed orange, embedded bone slivers and pieces form an intriguing mosaic. Try jiggling the pieces to make sure they are firmly attached.

SECURE BACKS: Sometimes flimsy cardboard is used to secure the backs of mirrors. Make sure to flip the mirror over to check the quality.

HUMIDITY: If you anticipate using the mirror in a bathroom, wood or maillechort versions are best. Brass, nickel, and copper mirrors will tarnish quickly when exposed to humid conditions.

ATTACHMENTS: Look for mirrors with attachments on the back side, especially if you want to hang your mirror. If there are no attachments, ask your vendor to rig some for you.

Pottery

Pottery has been made and used in Morocco for around a thousand years. Thriving since the Middle Ages, the ceramics industry is one of the oldest and richest of the Moroccan handicraft traditions. This is despite a decline under the French protectorate, which introduced porcelain to Morocco, as well as the influx of Chinese porcelain. Fez has long been the heart of the Moroccan ceramics tradition and still holds the title as the country's most important center of pottery production. Most pottery is made in cooperatives or workshops that are often family affairs. Common items are tagines, bowls, platters, and pitchers, since these are most useful in the Moroccan kitchen. However, other ceramic creations include inkwells, butter jars, soap dishes, lamps, boxes, vases, and even sinks.

Pottery decoration can take many shapes and forms, as most potters will paint without a pattern, using only their memory and the gift of improvisation. Paint colors vary, although Fez is known for its blue-and-white pottery, and Tamegroute (a small village in the Moroccan Draa Valley) is known for its green and ochre pottery. Floral and geometric patterns feature heavily, with motifs such as stars, flowers, buds, zigzags, chevrons, concentric circles, medallions, paisleys, cross-hatching, and leaves, to name a few. Often, the centers of bowls are occupied by a star or a flower. Calligraphy or Arabic letters are occasionally found, too. In addition to traditional patterns, monochrome Moroccan ceramics have appeared on the market in recent years, with the emphasis placed on color and

glazing rather than pattern. These plainer ceramics are sometimes decorated with filigree.

TIPS FOR BUYING MOROCCAN POTTERY

TAGINE USE: Tagines are a fantastic addition to any foodie's kitchen, but only the plain terra-cotta ones may be employed for cooking directly on the stove. The painted, patterned tagines are only for serving.

TOXINS: Metallic pottery is not safe to serve hot foods in. It should be reserved for decorative purposes only.

HANDMADE NATURE: Moroccan pottery is almost entirely handmade. Accordingly, matched sets are difficult to find, and glazing may not always be entirely similar.

SHIPPING: Moroccan pottery rarely survives shipping unless it is specially packed in a wooden crate of the appropriate size. It's best to hand-carry any ceramics found in the souks.

Poufs and Cushions

A Moroccan pouf is the equivalent of an ottoman. Poufs are versatile furniture items and perform comfortably as seats, footstools, and small tables. They can be found most everywhere in Morocco and, indeed, you don't have to try hard to spy small groups of men stooped over their pieces of leather, a cardboard template ready in hand to mark out each panel for their poufs. The panels are then sewn together by hand or by machine. Poufs can be purchased stuffed or unstuffed.

Moroccan poufs come in various materials, shapes, colors, and patterns. Three animal hides are commonly used: sheep, goat, and cow. Additionally, poufs may be made out of fabric, often muslin or striped Moroccan sabra (cactus silk). Round and square poufs are standard, but sometimes other shapes make a showing, such as rectangles. Yellow, orange, and brown leather poufs are the most colorfast, but poufs now come in a spectrum of shades, from electric blue to bright fuchsia. Metallic shades, particularly gold and silver, are very popular. While some poufs are simple and smart, others are elaborately decorated with images of stars (of Morocco and of David) or geometric patterns in the quasicrystalline style. Patterns are typically embossed on leather or embroidered on leather or fabric.

In addition to poufs, there are plenty of pretty Moroccan cushions to choose from. Striped cushion covers made out of sabra populate the medina. In upscale shops, there are embroidered versions, many featuring Rabat floral embroidery designs on muslin. Vintage flat-weave cushions of the Zaiane, Zaer, Beni M'Guild, and Beni M'Tir tribes are particularly ethnic; these are typically long and rectangular with a striped weave on one side and a highly patterned weave on the other. Leather and suede cushions in several colors can also be found in the souks. Cushions may be sold stuffed or unstuffed, depending on the seller and the type.

TIPS FOR BUYING MOROCCAN POUFS AND CUSHIONS

SMELL: The strong odor that used to accompany some Moroccan sheep hides has been largely remedied, but it's still worth having a sniff inside the pouf or cushion. If it smells odd, don't buy it. The smell will never go away, even with airing.

COLOR: If you can see subtle swirls of color on the leather pouf or cushion, then it has likely been surface-dyed. Make sure the leather has been fully dyed at the tannery and has a uniform tint.

STITCHING: You can tell whether a leather pouf or cushion is man-made or machine-made by examining the stitching from the inside. Stitching by hand leaves small gaps between the stitches, unlike the adjoining stitches of machines.

METALLICS: Many metallic poufs are actually vinyl, not leather. Make sure to ask your vendor and double-check yourself.

CLOSURES: Most vintage woven cushions have no zippers or buttons. You simply stuff them through a small opening and sew them shut.

STUFFING: The majority of poufs are sold unstuffed in the souks, making them easy to pack. Stuff them with inexpensive bed pillows or even old clothing.

Tea Glasses

The popularity of Moroccan mint tea means that tea glasses play a starring role in any Moroccan house. Unwilling to settle for one or two designs, artisans have created many styles, with a glass to suit every persona, from the purist to the diva. Glasses are often sold in sets of six, but upscale varieties can be bought singly.

One of the most popular and least expensive types of tea glass is the plain chauffeur glass, with a protruding glass ring around its middle, ostensibly designed to slot into the holders carried in some tea establishments. More upscale versions are similar to lusterware, each glass a brilliant, burnished shade. But there are far more ornate varieties of tea glasses, too. There is the typical but fanciful Arabian style, with designs applied via decal; these come most frequently in blues, reds, whites, and golds. Other glasses have hand-painted designs, replete with delicate swirls and twirls or images of folkloric figures in Moroccan clothing. Metal makes a showing, too, via filigreed flourishes soldered on each glass or hammered metal cups designed to slide onto the base of the glass to dress it up. Glasses with sandblasted geometric designs, new to the Moroccan marketplace, are very pretty. And speaking of sand, there are glasses with patterns formed in colored sand, a subtle reminder of the nearby desert.

TIPS FOR BUYING MOROCCAN TEA GLASSES

Decals: Glasses with designs applied by decal may be pretty, but they are not hard-wearing. Run your fingers over the surface to see if you can detect a subtle decal surface.

Imports: Be aware that not every Moroccan tea glass is artisanal or Moroccan. Some glasses—particularly the more complicated patterns and frostings—are factory-made in Turkey, and the Chinese have also gotten in on the action with their copies of Moroccan tea glasses.

Shipping: Tea glasses are unlikely to survive shipping from Morocco, unless packed with other goods in a container. Be prepared to carry them in your hand luggage.

Fragility: No matter the style of tea glass, as with all good things, they will come to an end (in this case with a slip of a hand). Make sure to buy extra.

Textiles

Morocco offers many wonderful textiles. Along with Moroccan carpets and Moroccan lanterns, textiles are the most useful items to infuse a home with exotic chic in the wink of an eye. Particularly worthwhile items include hanbels, handiras, and sabras.

HANBELS: Tucked away in corners of rug shops are stacks of beautiful vintage Moroccan blankets, known as hanbels. These are heavy and warm, normally made entirely of wool. Sizing varies, but quite a few are longer than a typical blanket. Hanbels can be plain but are more often striped in a wide variety of colors. Some include brocaded or pile elements or other decorative details. New blankets in conventional sizes and natural colors can also be purchased, many with fanciful large pom-poms on two sides.

HANDIRAS: There is also a variety of vintage Moroccan capes or handiras available. These are rectangular woven textiles with two woven cords used as ties. Handiras can be used as throws on the back of a couch, as carpets under tables, and in bedrooms at the foot of the bed. They are traditionally cream, ivory, and ecru, but some feature other colors. There are often bands of bushy cotton fringe or patterned stripes on the front or the back. Sequins add a glamorous touch to some handiras, often referred to as Moroccan wedding capes or wedding blankets.

SABRAS: Many Moroccan souks contain lengths of thick glossy cloth, known as sabras. While sabra itself is said to be cactus silk, more than one material may be mixed in to variegate the textures, such as stripes of chenille or linen. Although sabras can be monochromatic, more often they have energetic striping. No two cloths are the same, as each is an individual, handmade design. They come in a few sizes and can function as throws, bedspreads, and curtains.

TIPS FOR BUYING MOROCCAN TEXTILES

HOLES AND STAINS: Many hanbels and handiras are vintage and thus may have seen some wear. Accordingly, be on the lookout for discolorations and holes.

POLYESTER: Sabra is ostensibly made from cactus silk but is sometimes merely handwoven polyester. New handiras also may contain mixed fibers, including polyester.

SEQUINS: Small sequins—rather than large ones—on handiras generally indicate an older piece. Tarnishing can also be a clue to an older, more authentic piece.

WASHABILITY: Sabras generally wash very well and may be thrown in the machine. Wool blankets are best spot-cleaned and occasionally dry-cleaned.

chapter 10

FINDING DECOR AND EXPERTISE

When I was designing, building, and decorating Peacock Pavilions, I was lucky enough to have many resources at my fingertips. Closest to home (literally!) is my architect husband, who has studied Moroccan architecture extensively and has worked on Moroccan-inspired villas, riads, and inns in Morocco and farther afield. I also came to fill my Rolodex with a roster of craftspeople (both local and in the United States) well versed in the finishes and applications that I wanted for my own home. And there are the many stores where I shop for our interiors; they offer Moroccan lighting, textiles, pottery, furniture, and so much more.

234

Moroccan Home Goods

Naturally, Morocco itself is the very best source for all things Moroccan. As Marrakesh is the city I know best, several of the boutiques and stores I recommend are based in my adopted hometown. My secret hope is that this book will inspire you enough to plan your own trip to Marrakesh. However, I realize that a voyage to Morocco might not be in the cards for everyone, and so I have assembled an annotated list of design resources in Morocco and beyond. I have included a diverse group of vendors and specialists from the United States, Canada, Europe, and Australia. After all, a plane ticket should not stop you from living with Moroccan style.

AUSTRALIA

CARAVAN INTERIORS
85 Hall Street
2026 Sydney
+61-2-9365-0500

This is the closest thing to an Arabian love nest you will find in Bondi. All the merchandise in this alluring store travels from the Middle East and Asia. Caravan offers an array of home decor, glassware, hand-beaded bedsheets, and embroidered fabrics.

PURE AND GENERAL
114 Brougham Street
Potts Point
NSW 2011
+61-2-9360-6060
mail@pureandgeneral.com
www.pureandgeneral.com

This brand-new shop in Sydney started off on the right foot, with a packed shipping container full of goodies imported from Morocco and around the world. Stools, blankets, rugs, utensils, and more provide shoppers with plenty of items with which to create Moroccan interiors.

TABLE TONIC
+61-414-508-473
www.tabletonic.com.au

Table Tonic, run by Louise Bell, carries an assortment of textiles, jewelry, and smaller home accessories for bohemian chic environments, including poufs and other Moroccan objects.

CANADA

LE MARRAKECH STORE
3920, rue Saint-Denis
Montreal, Quebec, H2W 2M2
(514) 499-1953
info@lemarrakechstore.com
www.lemarrakechstore.com

Le Marrakech Store offers rare pieces from cities across Morocco. They sell to design professionals and to individuals, and many of their products are also available to rent.

PALMYRA DESIGN
4030 Derry Road West
Burlington, Ontario L7M 0R5
(905) 332-5254
info@palmyradesign.com
www.palmyradesign.com

Palmyra Design carries Moroccan goods with an emphasis on high quality. They shop personally for all of their merchandise; make sure to call before visiting.

FRANCE

CARAVANE
6, rue Pavée
75004 Paris
+33-1-44-61-04-20
caravane@caravane.fr
www.caravane.fr

This beautiful boutique carries all sorts of ethnic products with Moroccan inspiration mixed in, including tableware, lighting, textiles, and furniture, with an emphasis on the natural and the textural. If my pocketbook allowed, I would buy many things here!

MUSKELIL
contact@muskelil.com
www.muskelil.com

Valentina Pilia and Cassandra Karinsky are hip photo stylists and interior decorators selling unique Moroccan objects and carpets through their website. They have both lived in Marrakesh, but Muskelil is based in Paris.

GERMANY

L'ARTISAN
Kleinkölnstrasse 18
52062 Aachen
+49-241-88-80-73-09
info@l-artisan.de
www.l-artisan.de

L'Artisan features a wide range of unique handmade products from Morocco, including mirrors, chests, sofas, lighting, and tables. Because of their connections with artists and craftspeople, they are able to offer their goods at affordable prices.

KHMISSA MOROCCO DESIGN
Kazmairstrasse 33
D-80339 München
+49-89-74-37-19-70
info@khmissadesign.com
www.khmissadesign.com

Khmissa Morocco Design sells a nice collection of Moroccan lighting, furniture, accessories, textiles, and antiques at their shop in Munich. The owner searches for the best quality and also for vintage Moroccan one-of-a-kind treasures.

LE MARRAKECH
Kellerbleek 10
22529 Hamburg
+49-40-57-14-53-01
info@lemarrakech.de
www.lemarrakech.eu

This Hamburg shop offers a wide range of cement tiles in many colors, furniture, home accessories, and other Moroccan products.

MOROCCO INTERIORS
Leonhardtstrasse 3
14057 Berlin
+49-179-748-5705 or +49-30-21-80-66-81
+49-721-151435278 (fax)
www.morocco-interiors.com

This Berlin shop carries classic Moroccan housewares, including lanterns, wrought-iron furniture, tile tables, sabras, and more.

MOROCCO

AKKAL
219 Z.I. Sidi Ghanem
Route de Safi
Marrakesh
+212-5-24-35-60-24
+212-5-24-35-60-25 (fax)
akkal@menava.ma
www.akkal.ma

The word *akkal* comes from the Berber dialect and means "earth." It is no surprise then that this stylish ceramics shop sells an incredible range of earthenware products in sleek shapes and playful colors. Over the years, I have purchased many things at Akkal.

AYA'S MARRAKECH
11 bis, Derb Jdid, Bab Mellah
Marrakesh
+212-5-24-38-34-28 (phone and fax)
info@ayasmarrakech.com
www.ayasmarrakech.com

A small boutique run by a designer, this hidden shop is best known for its hand-embroidered tunics, but it sells everything that is beautiful.

BEN RAHAL
28, rue de la Liberté
Marrakesh
+212-5-24-43-32-73

Head to Sarmi Mohamed Taieb's shop to purchase some of the city's most beautiful carpets. Here you can find your very own antique Berber carpet amid the exclusive selection of rugs.

CÔTÉ SUD
4, rue de la Liberté
Marrakesh
+212-5-24-43-84-48

Belgian designer Sabine Bastin creates Moroccan goods with a European twist. Treat yourself to fabulous tableware, hand-painted tea glasses, and darling cushions and towels.

KIFKIF
8, Derb Laksour
Marrakesh
+212-6-61-08-20-41
kifkifbystef@gmail.com
www.kifkifbystef.com

Venture to Stephanie Benetiere's boutique for Moroccan products with a Western touch. Among the many gorgeous items, you will find the shop's signature products: leather bags, fun jewelry, and pretty glassware, many designed by Stephanie herself.

L. LANDON
294 2.I. Sidi Ghanem
Marrakesh
+212-6-63-72-70-02
laurence.landon@gmail.com
www.laurencelandon.com

Laurence Landon is a very talented and charming French designer of lovely things, including mirrored lights and candleholders. Every shimmering piece is a limited edition with art deco flair. Some of her work can be found at Peacock Pavilions.

LILAH SPIRIT
8, Sidi Ghanem, 294
Marrakesh
+212-6-61-31-78-19
lilahsaida@yahoo.fr

Make your way over to French designer Corinne Bensimon's shop for a fantastic collection of Moroccan homewares and her Moroccan slippers made with Liberty fabrics, which are all the rage. Corinne provides very exacting interior design services, and many of the curtains and cushions at Peacock Pavilions were made under her guidance.

LUP31 DESIGN
1, rue Okba Bnou Nafia
Marrakesh
+212-5-24-39-00-08
www.lup31.com

Ludovic Petit is the brains behind this purple-walled shop in a secret place in the medina. His hand-embroidered lighting, dip-dyed curtain panels, and custom bedding have made him one of the most sought-after interior designers in the city, and his atelier is a hive of activity. He also has a shop in Paris, called Neighbors. Lup31 crystal-embroidered lanterns beautify a guest bedroom at Peacock Pavilions.

MICHI
19–21 Souk Lakhachbia
Marrakesh
+212-6-61-86-44-07
www.michi-morocco.com

This elegant little shop is run by a Moroccan-Japanese couple, which makes for a unique design aesthetic. The most sought-after items are their babouches, which are worlds better than the rows of uniform slippers found elsewhere in the medina.

MILOUD EL JOULI
Souk Charatine Talâa no. 48
Marrakesh
+212-5-24-42-67-16
meljouli@hotmail.com

Designer Miloud El Jouli runs a sleek boutique tucked away in the Souk Charatine. His store is a treasure trove for colorful tunics, Moroccan lanterns with a modern elegance, and soft leather poufs. They even create furniture made to order, and they'll handle the shipping for you.

MUSTAPHA BLAOUI
144, rue Bab Doukkala
Marrakesh
+212-5-24-38-52-40

Here you'll find many treasures, including elaborately decorated hands of Fatima, handmade lanterns, dowry chests from the Rif, rugs from southern Morocco, and rooms and rooms filled with goodies.

ORIENTALISTE
11 and 15, rue de la Liberté
Marrakesh
+212-5-24-43-40-74

These two must-see shops sell hand-painted perfume bottles along with the best artisanal perfume in the city. In one of their boutiques, you can also find an exciting selection of Oriental antiques and paintings.

PEAU D'ANE
297 Sidi Ghanem
Marrakesh
+212-5-24-33-65-50
info@peaudane.de
www.peaudane.com

Offering some of the highest-quality items in Marrakesh, this store is in the city's industrial zone. It sells lamps with hammered finishes, mirrors with intricate patterns, and furniture upholstered with Moroccan fabrics.

SCÈNES DE LIN
70, rue El Houria
Guéliz, Marrakesh
+212-5-24-43-61-08
bleumajorelle@menara.ma

If you are looking for beautiful linens, this is the place to go. Scènes de Lin offers fabrics by the yard as well as tablecloths, napkins, and even some stylish caftans and accessories. If you can't get enough of their designs, you can make use of their interior design service.

33 MAJORELLE
33, rue Yves Saint Laurent
Marrakesh
+212-5-24-314-195
33ruemajorelle@gmail.com
www.33ruemajorelle.com

Abutting the Majorelle Gardens, this is Marrakesh's newest one-stop emporium and not to be missed. You'll find the prettiest, freshest Moroccan homewares, as well as hand-embroidered tunics and scarves—all from a range of Moroccan or Marrakesh-based designers. French owner Monique Bresson has a curator's eye. Expect to pay a little more, but the quality is excellent. My favorite shop in the new city!

ZID ZID KIDS
252 Quartier Industrial Sidi Ghanem
Marrakesh
+212-5-24-33-53-07
www.zidzid.com

Zid Zid Kids creates the most adorable items for children. Designers Julie and Moulay are incredibly talented, and it's no surprise that they have won awards and created children's spaces in some of the world's most beautiful hotels. They are also incredibly down-to-earth and lovely in person.

THE NETHERLANDS

LE SOUK
Zuiderwouder Dorpsstraat 24
1153 PC Zuiderwoude
+31-6-19689930
info@soukshop.com
www.soukshop.com

Le Souk sells furniture, home and personal accessories, and items for babies and children bought from or inspired by the Middle East. Owner Danielle de Lange lives in the Netherlands but collects goods from all over the world that mix traditional with modern, including Moroccan goods.

ZENZA HOME ACCESSORIES
Utrechtsestraat 101
1017 VK Amsterdam
+31-20-4230070
Rechtstraat 70
6221 El Maastricht
+31-43-32577 44
info@zenza.nl
www.zenza.nl

Zenza carries a wide assortment of Moroccan, North African, and Middle Eastern–inspired pendant, table, and wall lamps and lanterns. Zenza has captured the attention of designers worldwide for their large selection of handmade lighting.

SPAIN

ARTESANÍA MARROQUI
+34-956-630-383 or +34-610-419-938
info@artesania-marroqui.com
www.artesania-marroqui.com

Artesanía Marroqui is an online shop with a warehouse located in Algeciras, one of the main Spanish towns close to Morocco. Owners Antonio de La Varga and Nadia Hamada have supplied shops and decorated hotels in southern Spain, Portugal, and Morocco.

BARAKA
C. canvis vells, 2
Barcelona 08003
+34-932-684-220
baraka@barakaweb.com
www.barakaweb.com

This Barcelona shop carries Moroccan crafts, books, music, perfumes, and kitchenwares that have been purchased directly from the craftspeople of Fez, Marrakesh, Safi, Essaouira, Chefchaouen, the Atlas Mountains, and the Rif.

DECORACIÓN ANDALUSÍ
Urb Paraíso Barronal s/n
Ctra N 340 Km 167
Estepona 29680 Málaga
+34-952-884-215
+34-699-915-863
www.decoracion-andalusi.com

Decoración Andalusí specializes in custom Andalusian art and craftsmanship. They offer personalized design and decoration, furniture made to order, forged iron products, wood cabinetry, lighting, doors, and ceramic mosaics.

KASBAH
Urb. La Rumina, Local 5
Paseo del Mediterráneo, 443
Mojacar Playa
Almeria 04638
+34-950-473-036
info@kasbah.es
www.kasbah.es

Kasbah offers a unique and constantly evolving collection of handmade home furnishings and gifts. The majority of their merchandise is sourced from Morocco and Tunisia, but they also stock products from throughout the Arab world.

SWEDEN

CASA MARRAKECH
Östra Tullgatan 5
211 28 Malmö
+46-40-12-82-25
info@casamarrakech.se
www.casamarrakech.se

Casa Marrakech sells Moroccan blankets, tabletop items, furniture, lanterns, and tile.

SPITI
Sveavägen 64
111 34 Stockholm
+46-8-21-73-20
info@spiti.se
www.spiti.se

Spiti is a Swedish online shop with a storefront in Stockholm. They carry a wide selection of Eastern-inspired goods, along with some nice rustic contemporary items.

UNITED KINGDOM

BERBER INTERIORS
Bayfield Brecks
Cley Road
Holt
Norfolk NR25 7DZ
+44-1263-715555 or +44-1263-715624
enquiries@berberinteriors.com
www.berberinteriors.com

Berber Interiors was conceived by owner John Pryor during a visit to Morocco. It sells a nicely edited group of Moroccan housewares, with a lovely showroom in a traditional Norfolk barn.

BOHO GARDEN
38 Kensington Gardens
Brighton
East Sussex BN1 4AL
+44-1273-567642
info@boho-garden.com
www.boho-garden.com

This new shop in Brighton carries a selection of Moroccan frames, mirrors, lamps, vases, tableware, and other decorations.

DAR INTERIORS
Studio 3T, Cooper House
2 Michael Road
Fulham
London SW6 2AD
+44-20-7731-6388
+44-20-7731-8216 (fax)
info@darinteriors.com
www.darinteriors.com

An anthropologist and a designer joined forces to start Dar Interiors. They carry Moroccan tiles, furniture, fountains, lighting, ironwork, and hand-painted wooden pieces crafted in workshops that they have established in Morocco.

FEZ
71 Golborne Road
North Kensington
London W10 5NP
+44-20-8964-5573

Originally from Morocco, Omar Serroukh lives in London, where he runs his shop, Fez. The shop is located in a community called Little Morocco, where you can find several independent Moroccan businesses clustered together.

GRAHAM AND GREEN
+44-845-130-6622
mailorder@grahamandgreen.co.uk
www.grahamandgreen.co.uk

While they have many Moroccan pieces, Graham and Green's offerings are truly contemporary in nature, proving that Moroccan style can mix easily with the modern home. Visit their website for London store locations.

IDYLL HOME
enquiries@idyllhome.co.uk
www.idyllhome.co.uk

This stylish online shop carries an eclectic mix of home furnishings from around the world. They have a lovely range of ceramic patterned

Fez bowls, made from red clay in Morocco, as well as other Moroccan items.

KAZZBAR
Unit 1-2 Hamlyn House
Mardle Way
Buckfastleigh
Devon TO11 0NS
+44-800-288-8624
www.kazzbar.co.uk

Kazzbar sells everything from lanterns and slippers to leather poufs and rugs. You can even buy a sack of pouf stuffing, approximately 17.5 pounds (8 kg) of real sheeps' wool, for just £15.

MAROQUE
Unit 2E, Williamsport Way
Lion Barn Industrial Estate
Needham Market
Ipswich, IP6 8RW
+44-1449-723133
sales@maroque.co.uk
www.maroque.co.uk

Maroque sells Moroccan merchandise, including furniture, lanterns, ceramics, food ingredients, and bath products. Their website has information on how to achieve a Moroccan look, tips for entertaining, and recipes. Maroque sells items online and at their warehouse (call before visiting).

MEDINA MADNESS
Kohima
10 Shenfield Crescent
Brentwood
Essex CM15 8BN
+44-1277-213867
www.medinamadness.com

Medina Madness imports and sells gorgeous Moroccan Darhani candles. The owners' mission is to capture the scents of Morocco and encapsulate them in the most organic and eye-catching way possible.

MOROCCAN BAZAAR
Unit 2B and 2C
Kelvin Industrial Estate
Long Drive
Greenford
Middlesex UB6 8WA
+44-20-8575-1818
+44-20-8575-9426 (fax)
info@moroccanbazaar.co.uk
www.moroccanbazaar.co.uk

Moroccan Bazaar has been supplying Moroccan furnishings to retail stores and to the trade since 1970, but they also sell to the public at their showroom. They carry lighting, furniture, accessories, textiles, and outdoor products.

NIKI JONES
Unit 13 D8
Anniesland Business Park
Netherton Road
Glasgow G13 1EU
+44-141-959-4090
enquiries@niki-jones.co.uk
www.niki-jones.co.uk

With an emphasis on the handcrafted, Jones offers a range of ethically sourced housewares that are inspired by many different countries, including Morocco. The shop also carries many beautiful products of their own design.

PARMA LILAC
+44-20-7912-0882
info@parmalilac.co.uk
www.parmalilac.com

Parma Lilac sells products that are modern and simple. Many of their designs are Middle Eastern–influenced and have textural or visual elements that are reminiscent of Morocco. They have a showroom in West London near Portobello Road Market; visits are by appointment only.

PLUMO
+44-844-557-3590 (orders)
+44-208-889-9945 (customer service)
contact@plumo.com
www.plumo.com

Plumo carries original artistic clothing and household items. A number of their items are made in Morocco, and all would fit in nicely with a Moroccan interior. Although this website is based in the United Kingdom, Plumo shows prices in pounds, euros, and U.S. dollars and ships worldwide.

SARAH RAVEN
+44-845-092-0283
info@sarahraven.com
www.sarahraven.com

Go to this online kitchen and garden shop for Moroccan bowls in a rainbow of colors as well as for pretty mint tea glasses.

YASHAR BISH
96 Gloucester Road
North Laine
Brighton
East Sussex BN1 4AP
+44-1273-671900
www.yashar-bish.com

Yashar Bish is a shop packed full of carpets, kilims, cushions, tribal textiles, village artifacts, lamps, and curiosities from Asia Minor, Central Asia, and the Middle East.

UNITED STATES

ANTHROPOLOGIE
(800) 309-2500
www.anthropologie.com

Anthropologie is the perfect go-to store for housewares with a modern bohemian vibe. There is plenty of Moroccan influence at every turn, including in brightly painted pottery, cheery printed bedspreads, and even

decorative hardware with Moroccan detailing. With shops across the United States (and now in Europe), as well as online shopping and international shipping, you can get a little Moroccan fix anytime.

BADIA DESIGN
5420 Vineland Avenue
North Hollywood, CA 91601
(818) 762-0130
(818) 761-5042 (fax)
info@badiadesign.com
www.badiadesign.com

Badia Design carries Moroccan lighting, furniture, tiles, architectural elements, textiles, and accessories for sale in their showroom and online. They also have products, including tents, available for Moroccan-themed party rentals.

BERBER TRADING
2622 North Miami Avenue
Miami, FL 33127
(305) 572-0118
www.berbertrading.com

Berber Trading is owned and run by a former doctor and economist fascinated by the world of souk craftsmanship. The products are primarily from Morocco and are available for purchase online and at their Miami showroom.

CASBAH DECOR
(813) 263-8766
casbahdecor@yahoo.com
www.casbahdecor.com

Casbah Decor is an online store that sells everything from Moroccan architectural pieces to Moroccan tea sets. They have a wide range of furniture and textiles from Morocco.

CIRCA TRADING
info@circatrade.com
www.circatrade.com

The Harvard-educated owner of Circa Trading is a world traveler, and it shows in her curated collection. Her one-of-a-kind artisanal pieces and oddities have cultural significance to the places they are from, including Morocco. This is one of my favorite stores.

CURREY & COMPANY
50 Best Friend Road
Atlanta, GA 30340
(877) 768-6428
(678) 533-1499 (fax)
info@curreyco.com
www.curreyandcompany.com

Gorgeous lighting is the name of the game at Currey & Company. The selection is enormous and includes several Moroccan-inspired pieces. Expect only the very best quality.

DIA LIVING
(888) 407-8562
info@dialiving.com
www.dialiving.com

Featuring unique Moroccan-inspired designs, Dia Living offers handmade textiles that mix modern and vintage techniques in their online shop. They collect their designs from all over the world, including Africa, Asia, Europe, the Middle East, and South America.

FERROL STUDIO
(206) 370-2410
linda@ferrolstudio.com
www.ferrolstudio.com

Ferrol Studio sells goods that are often found in Morocco, such as olive oil soap, hammered silver bowls, and woven market baskets. Linda Ferrol's lifelong dream was to move from her home in Amsterdam to the United States and start a business; this is the realization of that dream.

JOHN DERIAN COMPANY
Decoupage & Imported Goods
6 East 2nd Street
New York, NY 10003
(212) 677-3917
(212) 677-7197 (fax)
shop@johnderian.com
www.johnderian.com

John Derian Company curates a wide variety of fascinating housewares and curiosities, both new and antique. Derian has spent a great deal of time in Morocco, and his stores often carry Moroccan goods, such as poufs, carpets, and lanterns. Items can be purchased at one of their three shops, over the phone, or at a number of retailers throughout the world.

JOHN DERIAN DRY GOODS
Textiles, Furniture, Rugs, and Art
10 East 2nd Street
New York, NY 10003
(212) 677-8408
drygoods@johnderian.com
www.johnderian.com

JOHN DERIAN NEW ENGLAND
Law Street (back of 396 Commercial Street)
Provincetown, MA 02657
(508) 487-1362
www.johnderian.com

MARTYN LAWRENCE BULLARD
8101 Melrose Avenue, Suite 205
Los Angeles, CA 90046
(323) 655-5080
(323) 655-5090 (fax)
info@martynlawrencebullard.com
www.martynlawrencebullard.com

Interior designer Martyn Lawrence Bullard has collections of fabric, furniture, rugs, and candles on the market in showrooms all over the world. Recent collections feature gorgeous Moroccan-inspired patterns and colors.

MOSAIK INTERIORS

7378 Beverly Boulevard
Los Angeles, CA 90036
(323) 525-0337
(323) 525-0341 (fax)
mosaik@e-mosaik.com
www.e-mosaik.com

Mosaik offers furniture, rare vintage caftans, Moorish antiques, tribal art, and handicrafts imported from Morocco. Everything they carry in their store is for sale and for rent.

SAHARA DESIGNS
U.S. and Canada Sales
(858) 571-3500
(858) 571-3533 (fax)
contact@saharadesigns.com
www.saharadesigns.com

Sahara Designs carries all types of Moroccan tiles, as well as architectural elements such as fountains and doors. They are based in California and Morocco; they ship throughout the world.

SAINT TROPEZ BOUTIQUE
25 Evelyn Way
San Francisco, CA 94127
(415) 702-9617
(415) 871-2188 (fax)
sales@sainttropezboutique.us
www.sainttropezboutique.us

Selling tile, textiles, lighting, and architectural elements, Saint Tropez Boutique aims to educate the public about the importance of craftsmanship and about Islamic architecture.

SHEHERAZADE
121 Orchard Street
New York, NY 10002
(212) 539-1771
(212) 539-1774 (fax)
info@sheherazadehome.com
www.moroccan-decor-furniture.com

Sheherazade sells furniture and accessories sourced from countries throughout the Mediterranean and

the Middle East, including Morocco. They also rent out furniture and other items for parties.

TAZI DESIGNS
333 Linden Street
San Francisco, CA 94102
(415) 503-0013
info@tazidesigns.com
www.tazidesigns.com

Tazi Designs is an import/export company that sells Moroccan goods and provides design services for its clients. They specialize in modern ethnic products and, in addition to smaller items, carry antique doors and Moroccan fountains.

WEST ELM
(888) 922-4119
www.westelm.com

West Elm knows just how to bring Moroccan flair into the twenty-first century. This brand has a great knack for interpreting Moroccan designs in new and fresh ways. Look for carpets with Moroccan patterns, Moroccan embroidery on bedding and cushions, and affordable Moroccan lanterns (among other items). There are stores across the United States, so you should have no problem being able to see and touch the merchandise before purchasing it.

WUNDERLEY
(724) 850-9616
sales@wunderley.com
www.wunderley.com

Wunderley sells a wealth of Moroccan products online and in several showrooms in the South. Their site has stunning furniture in particular.

MULTINATIONAL

EMERY & CIE

Emery & Cie creates beautiful tile, tableware, wallpaper, and furniture inspired by Morocco's patterns and colors. They have showrooms in several European cities.

BELGIUM
Reynders Straat, 20
2000 Antwerp
+32-3-231-30-84
antwerpen@emeryetcie.com
www.emeryetcie.com

27, rue de L'Hopital
1000 Brussels
+32-2-513-58-92
brussels@emeryetcie.com
www.emeryetcie.com

FRANCE
18, passage de la Main d'Or
75011 Paris
+33-1-44-87-02-02
paris@emeryetcie.com
www.emeryetcie.com

UNITED KINGDOM *(by appointment)*
c/o Retrouvious
1016 Harrow Road
London NW10 5NR
+44-20-8969-0222
london@emeryetcie.com
www.emeryetcie.com

HABIBI INTERIORS

Habibi Interiors carries tiles as well as customized preassembled fireplaces, fountains, and sinks. They have two locations in London and one in Oslo, Norway.

NORWAY
Gabels Gate 5
Oslo 0272
Anne@habibi-interiors.no
www.habibi-interiors.no

UNITED KINGDOM
1c, Greyhound Road
London NW10 5QH
+44-208-960-9203
+44-208-960-9223 (fax)
info@habibi-interiors.com
www.habibi-interiors.com

328 Wandsworth Bridge Road
London SW6 2TZ
+44-207-610-9944
+44-207-610-9940 (fax)
info2@habibi-interiors.com
www.habibi-interiors.com

NATURA CASA

www.naturaselection.com

Natura is a chain of stores with many locations throughout Europe. They sell objects, clothing, and fashion accessories with an exotic, earthy, and natural vibe, including products with a Moroccan influence.

Specialists

These are my favorite architects, artisans, interior designers, and landscapers with experience in Moroccan design.

ARCHITECTS

CHRIS REDECKE
Peacock Pavilions,
Marrakesh, Morocco
+212-6-64-414653
c_redecke@yahoo.com
www.credecke.com

Walking the medinas of Morocco for the past ten years has influenced Chris's designs, and he has a keen design eye for Moroccan-inspired architecture. In addition to having designed Peacock Pavilions, he has completed designs for riads and Moroccan corporate offices. Chris's projects span the globe from the United States to Namibia, Nepal, and Saudi Arabia. He maintains his architect's license in the United States, where he started his career practicing primarily residential design. Chris is available for Moroccan architectural design consultations anywhere in the world.

ARTISANS

The following artisans are all highly skilled experts at faux finishes and stenciling. Everyone listed has experience working with Moroccan designs, has traveled to Morocco, and has contributed their design experience to Peacock Pavilions.

ARTISTIC FINISHES BY VICKI
Vicki Schultz
tikipaints@hotmail.com
www.finishesbyvicki.com

ARTWORKS SPOKANE
Nancy Jones
www.artworksspokane.com
info@artworksspokane.com

This company specializes in tadelakt.

BOHEMIAN SPIRIT FAUX ART
Gwen Ware
gwen@bohemianspirit.com
www.bohemianspirit.com

CYNTHIA DESIGNS
Cynthia Davis
cynthia@cynthiadesigns.com
www.cynthiadesigns.com

FAUX COUTURE
Robin Johnston
info@fauxcouture.net
www.fauxcouture.net

FAUX DESIGN STUDIO
Deborah Hayes
debbie@ilovefaux.com
www.ilovefaux.com

HEATHER BRUNO-SEARS
hbspaint@hotmail.com
www.heatherbrunosears.com

JON SUNDE
jon@jonsunde.com
www.jonsunde.com

Jon is a specialist in plasterwork and tadelakt.

KARI CALDWELL STUDIOS
Kari Caldwell
callkari2@sbcglobal.net

LULU PAINTING
Alicia Danzig
lulupainting@gmail.com
www.lulupainting.com

MARGARET VON KAENEL
krushm@sbcglobal.net
www.mvk-decoart.com

O'NEILL STUDIOS
Maggie O'Neill
info@oneillstudios.com
www.oneillstudios.com

PAM GRACE
pgrace@colouredpaint@aol.com
www.colouredpaint.com

REBECCA ROTH SOPHISTICATED SURFACES LLC
Rebecca L. Roth
beckpaints@yahoo.com

REBECCA HOTOP
rebeccapaints4u@aol.com
www.faux-finish-artistry.com

INTERIOR DESIGNERS

ANTONY TODD
52 East 11th Street
New York, NY 10003
(212) 367-7363
antonytoddhome@anthonytodd.com
www.antonytodd.com

With a background in set and floral design, Todd has a great eye for proportion and color. He decorates with a global style that is timeless.

JESSICA HELGERSON INTERIOR DESIGN

723 NW 18th Avenue
Portland, OR 97209
(503) 548-4984
(503) 467-4830 (fax)
interior@jhinteriordesign.com
www.jhinteriordesign.com

Jessica Helgerson works with a team of designers focused on using sustainable pieces in both home and business environments. Their designs are sophisticated but minimal and fresh, and they incorporate Moroccan and other Middle Eastern pieces.

SCOUT DESIGNS

(646) 330-4878
info@scoutdesigns.com
www.scoutdesignsnyc.com

The work of Scout Designs frequently includes an exotic twist, and they often incorporate Moroccan carpets from my own Red Thread Souk. Scout Designs is owned by Nicki Clendening and Callie Jenschke.

LANDSCAPE DESIGNERS

ANCIENT OLIVE TREES

(707) 953-8562
(800) 819-7795 (fax)
aaron@ancientolivetrees.com
www.ancientolivetrees.com

Ancient Olive Trees maintains an orchard of old-growth olive trees in California, which they sell for landscaping purposes. They provide everything from consultation to transportation to tree installation.

ARTERRA LANDSCAPE ARCHITECTS

88 Missouri Street
San Francisco, CA 94107
(415) 861-3100
(415) 861-3330 (fax)
www.arterrallp.com

Arterra Landscape Architects has experience designing Moorish and Moroccan-inspired gardens.

CHARLOTTE ROWE GARDEN DESIGN

118 Blythe Road
Brook Green
London W14 0HD
+44-20-7602-0660
design@charlotterowe.com
www.charlotterowe.com

Charlotte Rowe Garden Design offers garden design consultancy to clients—from small urban courtyards, gardens, and roof terraces to full-scale country landscaping. Rowe has experience working in the Moroccan style, and has been featured on my blog, *My Marrakesh*.

JEFFREY BALE GARDEN DESIGN

jeffreygardens@earthlink.net
www.jeffreygardens.com

Bale creates intricate hardscaping, such as walkways, patios, and steps, for his clients' gardens. He uses a technique called pebble mosaic, setting multicolored stones and pavers into very detailed patterns.

Suppliers

Here are some terrific sources for dyes/sealers, paints, stencils, tents, textiles, and tiles.

DYES/SEALERS

AMERICAN DECORATIVE CONCRETE
(816) 448-2036
sales@ameripolishdye.com
www.ameripolishdye.com

This company sells AmeriPolish, ColorJuice, and Dye-N-Seal, all used in staining and coloring cementitious surfaces.

COLORFAST INDUSTRIES, INC.
(817) 546-4910
sales@colorfastind.com
www.colorfastind.com

ColorFast is a brand of grout, caulking, and sealers for use with tile, woodworking, and painting.

COLORMAKER
Smart Surface Technology, Inc.
(604) 244-3122
www.colormakerfloors.com

Aquacolor, Colorfast, and DESO dye concentrates are all products by Colormaker, a source for decorative concrete supplies. These products are for use in staining concrete and can create a range of effects from a soft and subtle color wash to more brilliant hues.

STENCILS

ROYAL DESIGN STUDIO
(800) 747-9767 (orders)
(619) 934-9062
sales@royaldesignstudio.com
www.royaldesignstudio.com

Melanie Royals of Royal Design Studio has an amazing collection of Moroccan stencils that were designed for and used at Peacock Pavilions.

THE STENCIL LIBRARY
Stocksfield Hall
Stocksfield
Northumberland NE43 7TN
+44-1661-843-984
info@stencil-library.co.uk
www.stencil-library.co.uk

This British company designs and manufactures decorative and signage stencils that are sold through their website, by specialist retailers, and in their showroom. Check out their mosaic stencils selection, or type in search term "Moroccan."

TENTS

ARABIAN TENTS
Upper Tilton Barn, Firle, nr Lewes
East Sussex BN8 6LL
+44-800-88-15-229
info@arabiantents.com
www.arabiantents.com

This company provides themed tents and furnishings to rent for parties and weddings. With such colorful names as Arabian, Moulin Rouge, and Peacock, each style has its own unique, exotic look.

WHITE CANVAS
+44-1749-899255
enquiries@whitecanvastents.com
www.whitecanvastents.com

White Canvas carries a range of tents available for rent or for purchase.

Their eponymous white canvas tents provide a perfect backdrop upon which to create any type of Moroccan ambiance.

TEXTILES

KATHRYN IRELAND
LOS ANGELES SHOWROOM
636 North Almont Drive
West Hollywood, CA 90069
(310) 246-1906

LONDON SHOWROOM
Fairbanks Studio 2
65–69 Lots Road
London SW10 0RN
+44-20-7751-4554
+44-20-7751-4555 (fax)
info@kathrynireland.com
www.kathrynireland.com

Kathryn Ireland designs and makes fabrics that are a bohemian mix of Mexican and Moroccan. *House Beautiful* has named her one of the top hundred designers in the United States.

MADELINE WEINRIB ATELIER
Madeline Weinrib
ABC Carpet & Home
888 Broadway, 6th floor
New York, NY 10003
(212) 473-3000, ext. 3780
(212) 228-1761 (fax)
contact@madelineweinrib.com
www.madelineweinrib.com

Madeline Weinrib is a painter and designer living in New York who creates fabrics with prints inspired by Morocco, India, and other exotic locales.

MOKUM

www.mokumtextiles.com

New Zealand–based Mokum offers a comprehensive collection of quality textiles for upholstered seating, walls, windows, and floor coverings. They have trade showrooms throughout Australia, New Zealand, and the United States.

RAOUL TEXTILES

Sally and Tim McQuillan
36 State Street
Santa Barbara, CA 93101
(805) 899-4947
(805) 899-4828 (fax)
www.raoultextiles.com

This family-owned business designs beautiful hand-printed textiles. Pattern interpretations are inspired by several different cultures, including Morocco.

TILE

ANN SACKS

(800) 278-8453
www.annsacks.com

Ann Sacks tiles bring elegance to any space. Look for the Medina, Kibak, Paccha, Coloured Earth, and Cotto Antiqua collections.

COUNTRY FLOORS

15 East 16th Street
New York, NY 10003
(212) 627-8300
(212) 242-1604 (fax)
info@countryfloors.com
www.countryfloors.com

Country Floors carries tiles for walls, floors, pools, and spas; for their most Moroccan-inspired tile, look for the collections named Alhambra, Baba Chic, La Brea Moresque, and Maroc.

FILMORE CLARK

607 West Knoll Drive
West Hollywood, CA 90069
(310) 652-6867
lee@filmoreclark.com
www.filmoreclark.com

Filmore Clark focuses on buying tiles that are made in the United States, but the inspiration for the tiles is global. Tiles from several different companies are brought together in one showroom curated by owner Lee Nicholson.

KHAIMA

Sterkrader Strasse 49–59
Höfe am Borsighafen
13507 Berlin
+49-30-21-01-69-62
info@khaima.de
www.khaima.de

Bodil Horstmann, the owner of this Berlin shop, specializes in tile (cement and enameled terra-cotta), kitchen and bathroom equipment, and mosaic tiles and tables. She also customizes client orders with Moroccan artisans she has worked with for years.

MARRAKECH DESIGN

info@marrakechdesign.se
www.marrakechdesign.se

With two locations in Sweden, Marrakech Design has a wide range of Moroccan-influenced floor and wall tiles.

MOSAIC HOUSE

32 West 22nd Street
New York, NY 10010
(212) 414-2525
(212) 414-2526 (fax)
contactus@mosaichse.com
www.mosaichse.com

Mosaic House has a huge selection of tile, including Moroccan tile. They make and carry mosaic tile, border tile, cement tile, and hand-painted tile for both indoor and outdoor use.

MOSAIC DEL SUR

info@mosaicdelsur.com
www.cement-tiles.es (cement tiles)
www.zellige-tiles.com (glazed tiles)
www.terrazzo-tiles.com (terrazzo)

Mosaic del Sur carries cement tiles, glazed tiles, and terrazzo. You can visualize your patterns with their online mosaic and terrazzo simulators.

POPHAM DESIGN

86, rue Sidi Ben Slimane
Marrakesh
+212-66-711-4572
contact@pophamdesign.com
www.pophamdesign.com

Caitlin and Samuel Dowe-Sandes moved to Morocco from the United States in 2006 and found inspiration in the tiles of their new home in the medina. They started sketching their own designs and opened their own business, focused on stylish Moroccan cement tiles. The majority of tiles at Peacock Pavilions are from Popham Design.

TABARKA STUDIO

(480) 968-3999
sales@tabarkastudio.com
www.tabarkastudio.com

Tabarka Studio is a producer and wholesaler of hand-painted decorative terra-cotta tiles.

TERRA HOME

(250) 335-3149
info@linguaterratile.com
www.linguaterratile.com

Terra Home specializes in handmade ceramic art tile and custom tile designs. Look at the Alhambra collection for tiles with Moorish influence. Terra Home is based in Denman Island, British Columbia, Canada, but they ship throughout North America.

Acknowledgments

Ah, writing and photographing a book. Who knew that it would require the help of so many?

A heartfelt thank you, *merci*, and *shoukran* to the following people, who allowed me into their homes: Corinne Bensimon, Delphine Warin and Souhail Tazi, Stephanie Hugon, Ludovic Petit, Rose Girardot, John Quinn, Helmut Sorge, Catherine Charpentier, Julie Klear and Moulay Essakalli, Yann Dobry, Rebecca Raft and Peter Conroy, Sylvain Breton, Geraldine Leymarie and David Schneuwly, Aurelia Tazi Haag and Sadek Tazi, Anne Favier, Nathalie Locatelli, Marie Charlotte Briastre, Kamal Laftimi, and Adriano Pirani.

Many thanks also to those who helped me with bits of book research, including Alex Bluett, Christiana Coop, Kaydee Dahlin, Chantal Hintze, Todd Oberndorfer, Lindsey Runyon, and Sarah Winward.

Thank you to the wonderful blogging community who shared their favorite Moroccan resources, including Courtney Barnes (stylecourt.blogspot.com); Holly Becker (decor8blog.com); Katie Denham (katie d-i-d.blogspot.com); Patricia Gray (patriciagrayinc.blogspot.com); Rochelle Greayer (greayer.com); Petra Hassan (ranipink.blogspot.com); Jeanine Hays (aphrochicshop.com); Jeska Hearne (lobsterandswan.com); Cassandra Karinsky (www.muskelil.com); Helena Karjalainen (roomservice.blogg.se); Carole King (deardesigner.co.uk); Erin Loechner (designformankind.com); Luciane (HomeBunch.com); Megan Morton (meganmorton.com); Di Overton (designersblock.blogspot.com); Kati Sarniña (www.delikatissen.com); Susan Serra (thekitchendesigner.org); Fabienne Serriere (fabienne.us); Ellie Tennant (homeshoppingspy.wordpress.com and Ideal Home Magazine); Jo Walker (desiretoinspire.net); and Joni Webb (cotedetexas.blogspot.com).

My gratitude goes to French photographer extraordinaire Delphine Warin, who showed me how to put my camera on manual and accompanied me as my assistant, model, and muse on many photo shoots. The portraits of my family and a few other shots are Delphine's work. I am also thankful to Martin Allen, who acted as my photography assistant for several shoots in Essaouira and Marrakesh.

I am especially grateful to Ingrid Abramovitch, who brought this project to Artisan, and for the deft touch of my editor, Judy Pray, and the creative eye of book designer Susan Baldaserini. A big thanks to everyone at Artisan: Ann Bramson, Sibylle Kazeroid, Nancy Murray, Trent Duffy, Allison McGeehon, Lia Ronnen, Molly Erman, Bridget Heiking, and Barbara Peragine. Special thanks are also due to Melanie Royals (royaldesignstudio.com) for her beautiful Moroccan patterns and to my literary agent, Jill Kneerim.

I am particularly indebted to my husband, Chris, and children, Skylar and Tristan, who put up with me through all the natural disasters and prolonged absences that go into writing and photographing a book. I promise to make it up to you.

Last but not least, my appreciation goes out to the city of Marrakesh, which stole my heart years ago. It's a love affair I've never regretted.

Index

Page numbers in *italics* refer to illustrations.

A

accessories:
    for bathrooms, 172, 174
    for bedrooms, 153–55
    for dining areas, 134–36, *135,*
        136
    for entries, 183
    for kitchens, *161,* 165
    for living areas, 124–27, *125*
Andalusian gardens, 26
Arabian Nights, The, 12, 222
arches, 26, *26, 44,* 45–46, *46, 173,*
    176

architects, 245
architecture, 20–111
    bedroom styles of, 140–49,
        143, 147
    color used in, 66–89, *70–71,*
        74–75, 86
    contemporary Moroccan,
        32–39, *32, 37*
    decorative finishes, 54–65,
        54–55, 56–57, 60–61, 64
    external influences on, 23–31,
        22, 25, 26, 30
    features of, 42–53, *44, 46, 47,*
        49, 50, 53

ARCHITECTURE (*cont.*)

fortresslike style of, 22, *22*

pattern and, 90–111, *92, 94–
    95, 96–97, 98, 100–101, 103,
    105, 106–7, 108*

artisans, sources of, 245

B

Bahia Palace, Marrakesh, *64*

banquette seating, *120,* 121, 122,
    123, 124, *130, 164, 189, 190,
    195, 196,* 202, 221

baraka, 13, 145, 169

bathrooms, 170–75, *171, 173*

    beauty treatments, 175

    home decoration of, 174

bedrooms, 138–57, *143, 147, 151,
    152*

    architectural styles and
        finishes, 140–49, *143, 147*

    furniture, surfaces, and
        accessories for, 150–55, *151,
        152*

    home decoration of, 144, 149,
        153

    how to make a headboard,
        156–57

beds, *51,* 146–49, *147, 148, 151,
    152, 171*

bedspreads, 147, *147,* 149, *151, 152*

bejmat tile, *37, 54,* 56, 57, 140,
    144, *164, 190,* 200

Bensimon, Corinne, *135, 148*

Berber tribes, 13, 102, 145, 156

    carpets, 77, 216

Bergé, Pierre, *75*

black and brown dyes and
    enamels, 80–81

black dess (polished cement),
    37, 54

blankets, handwoven, *71,* 126,
    143, 147, 148, 151, 233

blue dyes and enamels, 72–75,
    74–75

C

calligraphy, *53,* 98, *98, 143*

Casablanca, 30

ceilings, 64–65, *64,* 140, *143, 162*

    home decoration of, 65

cement tile, *37, 44, 49,* 56–58, *56,*
    60, 62, *92, 99,* 140–42, *143,
    164,* 165, 170, 176, 180, *190*

    how to install a floor with,
        58–59

Charpentier, Catherine, *32*

citrus trees, 203–4, *205*

color charting, 66–89, *70, 75, 86*

    blacks and browns, 80–81

    blues, 72–75, *75*

    dyers' souks, 86, *86*

    greens, 82–83

    home decoration with, 87, 144

    how to dye a concrete floor, 88–89

    Moroccan palette and, 70–85, *70*

    natural and synthetic dyes, 69

    reds, 78–79

    and symbolism in Moroccan culture, 73, 77, 79, 81, 83, 85

    whites, ivories, and beiges, 76–77

    yellows and oranges, 60, 84–85, *173*

construction materials, 44, *44*

courtyards, 33–36, *37*

cushions, *107, 125, 189, 195*

    tips on buying, 230

D

Dar Rumi, Marrakesh, *37, 60, 147, 151*

dars, *see* riads and dars

dess (polished cement), 54, *54*

dining areas, 130–36, *132, 135*

    accessories for, 134–36, *135*

    furnishings and seating for, 130–33, *132*

dining tables, 130, *132, 133, 135, 136, 162*

domes, 47, *47*

door knockers, buying tips for, 220

doors, *26, 39, 48, 49,* 68, 87, *92, 99, 142*

    tips for buying, 218

dyers' souks, 86, *86*

dyes, natural and synthetic, 69

E

embroidery, 105–9, *105, 107, 108, 181*

entryways, 176, *181,* 183

evil eye and genies, 13, 15

F

face mask recipe, 175

Fatima (cook), *161*

Fez, 73, 102, 225, 228

    embroideries of, 107, *107, 108, 196*

finishes, decorative, 54–56, *54, 56, 60, 64*, 140–49, *143, 147*

floors, 54–59, *54, 56*, 92, *94*

   bejmat tile, *37, 54*, 56, 57, *140, 144, 164, 190*

   black dess, *37, 54*

   cement, *51*

   cement tile, *37, 44, 49*, 56, 57, *58, 60, 62, 92*, 140–42, *143, 164*, 165, 176, 180, *190*

   home decoration of, 57

   how to dye concrete, 88–89

   how to stencil, 110

   patterned tile, *94*

floral patterns (tawriq), 24, *25, 93, 96, 96*

flowering plants, 206, *206*, 209

fountains, *22*, 24, *25, 39*, 53, *53*, 104, 200, 202

French influence in Morocco, 30, *30*

furnishings, 68, 104, *119, 120*, 122–23, 124, 128–29, *135, 171*

   for bedrooms, 150

   dining tables, 130, *132*, 133, *135, 136, 162*

   how to make a coffee table, 128–29

   how to make a headboard, 156–57

   how to make furniture polish, 137

   for outdoor living spaces, 186–89, *189*, 190–95, *190, 195*

   tables for coffee or tea, 122, 123, 133, 150, *151, 171, 189, 195*, 221

   tips for buying, 221

   see also banquette seating

furniture polish recipe, 137

G

gardens, 203–11, *205, 206, 208*

   flowering, 206, *206*, 209

   herbs, 208, *208*, 209, 210

   home decoration of, 209

   how to create a Moroccan herb garden, 210

   succulents and cacti, 205, *205*

   trees and, 203–4, *205, 206*

geometric patterns (tastir), 24, *25, 62, 93, 94, 94*, 195

geps (carved plaster), *26, 63, 65, 77, 92, 96*, 140, 146, *162*

green dyes and enamels, 82–83

H

haiks (handwoven fabric), 153

hair mask recipe, 175

hallways, 176, *176*, 180, *181*, 183

hammams (steam baths), 172

    beauty treatments, 175

    bowls, 226

hanbels, *see* blankets, handwoven

handiras (wedding blankets), *125*,

    147, *147*, 149, 152, 156–57,

    196, 233

Hassan II (king), 102

headboards, 104, *143*, 149, 152,

    156–57

herbs, 208, *208*, 209, 210

home decoration:

    of bathrooms, 174

    of bedrooms, 144, 149, 153

    of ceilings, 65

    of dining areas, 133

    of entries, hallways, and

        stairs, 183

    of floor surfaces, 57

    of gardens, 209

    of kitchens, 165

    of living areas, 123, 126

    with Moroccan color, 87

    with Moroccan embroidery, 109

    with Moroccan pattern, 99

    of outdoor spaces, 202

    of seating areas, 123

    with zellij tile, 104

home hardware, buying tips for,

    220

I

Ibn Hanbal, 24

interior designers, 245–46

K

kitchens, 158–59, *161*, *162*, *164*

    home decoration of, 165

Koutoubia Mosque, *46*

L

landscape designers, 246

lanterns, *39*, 62, 124, 126, 134,

    135, 136, *143*, 150, 153, *173*,

    175, *176*, *181*, 183, *189*, 190,

    195, 202

    tips on buying, 222–23

lighting, tips on buying, 222–23

Lilah Spirit, *148*, 190

living areas, 114–29, *119*, *120*, *125*

LIVING AREAS (cont.)

accessories for, 124–27, *125*

furnishings and seating for, *120*, 122–23

Moroccan salons, 121–22

in riads/dars, 116

M

magic, 12–13, 77, 145, 169

Majorelle, Jacques, 75, 87

Majorelle blue, 73, *75*, 87, 209

market baskets for storage, 183

tips on buying, 224

Marrakesh, 6–7, 30, 225

mashrabiya (turned wood or dowel work), 52, *53*, 146, *176*

medinas (old cities), 22, 33, 36, 40

dyers' souks in, 86

metalware, 99, 126, 183

tips on buying, 225–26

milk and butter, 169

mirrors, tips on buying, 227

Modello Designs, *143*

Moroccan home goods sources, 236–43

Moroccan mint tea recipe, 166

Moroccan salons, 121–22

Moroccan style, 18–211

bedrooms, 138–57, *143*, *147*, *151*, *152*

dining areas, 130–37, *132*, *135*

French influences on, 30, *30*

Islamic influences on, 23–25, *22*, *25*

kitchens, baths, and transitional spaces, 158–63, *161*, *162*, *164*, *171*, *173*, *176*, *181*, *182*

living areas, 112–29, *119*, *120*, *125*

outdoor living spaces and gardens, 184–211, *189*, *190*, *195*, *196*, *201*, *205*, *206*, *208*

sourcing of, 212–49

Spanish influence on, 26–27, *26*

Morocco, 6–17

Berber tribes of, 13, 77, 102, 145, 156, 216

evil eye and genies of, 13, 15

food and magical *baraka* in, 169

greetings important in, 9

history and culture of, 12–13

magic and weaving in, 145

snake charmers of, 16

mosques, 24, *25*, *46*

Muhammad the Prophet, 79, 81, 83, 172

Mustapha's Carpet Emporium, *119*

O

olive oil:
  face mask recipe, 175
  hair mask recipe, 175
olives and olive trees, 169, 204, *206*
outdoor living spaces, 184–202, *189, 190, 195, 196, 201*
  freestanding pergolas and tents, 196–99, *196*
  gardens, 203–11, *205, 206, 208*
  home decoration of, 202
  pools and fountains, 200–202, *201*
  roof terraces, 186–89, *189, 205*
  verandas and porches, 190–95, *190, 195*

P

palm groves, 203
patterns, 90–111, *94, 96, 98,* 150, *151,* 170 *182*

basics of, 93–99, *94, 96, 98*
home decoration with, 99, *104,* 109, *136,* 174
how to stencil a floor, 110
special applications of, 100–111
Peacock Pavilions, 8, *46, 47, 49, 56, 98, 125, 135, 164, 182, 196, 201,* 206, 210, 253
  guest rooms of, *51, 92, 119, 143*
Petit, Ludovic, *105, 108, 143,* 147, *181*
pools, 200–201, *201*
Popham Design, *56, 164*
pottery, 160, *161*
  tips on buying, 228–29
poufs/ottomans, 109, *119,* 122, 123, 130, *143, 147*
  tips on buying, 230

R

Rabat embroidery style, *105,* 107, *107*
red dyes and enamels, 78–79
Red Thread Souk, *135,* 253
riads and dars, 22, 32, 33–39, *37, 40, 48, 49,* 130, 140, 170, 180, 200

RIADS AND DARS (*cont.*)

kitchens in, 160–62, *161*
living areas in, 116, *120*
roof terraces, *44, 47,* 186–89, *189,*
205
roof tiles, 26
roses and rose products, *53, 201,*
206, *206,* 209
Royal Design Studio, *49, 50–51,*
110, *143, 182,* 196
Royals, Melanie, *98,* 110, *182, 196*
rugs, 87, 92, *120,* 124, *124,* 134,
135, 136, *143,* 147, 148, *149,*
150, *152, 153,* 171, *176, 181,*
196, 202
tips for buying, 216
understanding symbols on,
217

S

sabra cloth, 147, *147,* 149, 150,
152, 230, 233
saffron, 169
Saint Laurent, Yves, *75*
salt and *baraka,* 169
seating arrangements, *120,* 121–
23, 130, *132, 164,* 186–89,
189, 190, *195,* 196, 202, 221
souks, 86, *86,* 160

sourcing Moroccan style, 212–49
finding decor and expertise,
234–49
shopping for chic, 214–33
suppliers, 238–39
stairs, 176, 180, *182,* 183
stenciling, 65, 99, 110, 144, *182*
sources of, 248
succulents and cacti, 205, *205,*
209

T

tables for coffee or tea, 122, 123,
133, 150, *151, 171, 195*
tadelakt (surface applications),
47, 60, *60,* 62, 81, 142, *143,*
146, *151,* 152, *164, 170, 173,*
200
tagines, 165, 229
Tanjia restaurant, Marrakesh,
53, 135
Tazenakht carpets, 81, 150
tea glasses, tips on buying, 232
tents, dining or lounging, 196,
196
sources of, 248
textiles, *94,* 99
sources of, 248–49

tips on buying, 233

tiling, *22*, 23–24, *25*, *54–55*, 56–58,
56

   sources of, 249

V

verandas and porches, 190–95,
190, *195*

villas, 38–39, *39*, 116, *119*, 122–23,
162, 180, 190

Volubilis, 102

W

walls, 60–63, *60*, 68, *92*, *98*

   home decoration of, 62

   tadelakt treatments of, 60, 62,
81, 142, *143*, 151, 152, *164*,
173

   zellij mosaic tiling and, *100*,
102, *103*

Warin, Delphine, *120*, *195*

white dyes and enamels, 76–77

windows, 49–50, *49*, *51*, 142, *162*

   coffee tables made from,
128–29

   home decoration of, 144

   tips for buying, 218

Y

yellow and orange dyes and
enamels, 60, 84–85, *173*

Z

Zara Home, *151*

zellij mosaic tiling, *22*, 53, 60, 81,
92, *94*, 100, *100*, 102–4,
103, 133, 146, 162, 164, 165,
190

About the Author

Maryam Montague, born in Egypt to an American father and an Iranian mother, considers herself a citizen of the world. Her thirst for adventure and passion for humanitarian aid work has sent her to such countries as Iraq, Sri Lanka, Afghanistan, Pakistan, South Africa, and Mali. When Maryam isn't busy trying to save the world, she helps design it. Maryam and her architect husband designed, built, and decorated Peacock Pavilions, a boutique hotel on the outskirts of Marrakesh where they live with their two children. Maryam's eye for interior design has been featured on HGTV and the Travel Channel. Maryam's blog, *My Marrakesh,* has garnered millions of hits and has received attention from publications such as *National Geographic, Time.com, The Guardian, New York* magazine, *The New York Times,* and many more.

You can find out more about Maryam and her work at the following sources:

RED THREAD SOUK

Red Thread Souk is Maryam's online shop selling Moroccan goods. She specializes in Berber carpets, handira (wedding blankets), embroidered poufs, and other Moroccan housewares.
www.redthreadsouk.com

MY MARRAKESH

My Marrakesh is the blog Maryam started when she first moved to Marrakesh, and it continues today. On it you will find the inside story on life at Peacock Pavilions, information on interior design, and musings on good stuff in general. It was voted the Best African blog in the 2011 Annual Weblog Awards.
www.mymarrakesh.com

PEACOCK PAVILIONS

Peacock Pavilions is a boutique guesthouse in Marrakesh, nestled in an olive grove on the outskirts of the city. Designed by Maryam's architect husband, Chris, and decorated by Maryam herself, Peacock Pavilions offers two private guest pavilions, with a total of six double-occupancy rooms. There is also an outdoor cinema, a tiled pool, and a hand-painted Moroccan dining tent. Maryam conducts personal Moroccan shopping tours for guests and hosts retreats year round.
info@peacockpavilions.com
www.peacockpavilions.com